Effective Cover Letters - Secrets to Writing Great Cover Letters and Landing That Job!

101 World Class Expert Facts, Hints, Tips and Advice

on Resumes and Cover Letters

Information is power – you know that. But, how do you research the best Resumes and Cover Letters strategies, without spending too much of your time (and money) on it? The average person earns $ 1100 per week, which equates to $ 27 per hour. Trying to do the research yourself would take you at least 5 hours to come up with the best information, AND you'll have to do this on a regular basis to come up with the most up to date and current information.

There has to be a different way to find the info you want! Well, yes there is... we did all the research for you, combed through all the information and got down to the hard core of the 101 most up to date and best Facts, Hints, Tips and Advice here, in this book.

The 101 of the most current, most actual and beneficial Facts, Hints, Tips and Advice you can find from experts in the field on Resumes and Cover Letters:

Table of Contents

Resume Layout - Essential Tips to Get Started

If you are looking for advice on what constitutes an effective resume then you're off to a great start by choosing to read this. A resume is a critical component to finding a great job and the resume layout you choose will dictate how effective it is. It's easy to get lost in the sea of resume and job searching advice on the Internet, so let's start with the basics. Before diving into the specifics of what goes into a the document itself, it's important to first highlight and understand the goals of a successful resume. The overall goal of a resume is get an interview, plain and simple. It is meant to serve as an advertisement for you and allow you to get your "foot in the door" wherever you are applying to. Employers read through stacks of resumes wondering "Why should I hire this person?". They will scan your submission usually for no more than 30 seconds (often under 10) and then decide if it is worth their time to interview you. It is your job to convince them that they should, via your resume.

Similarly, a cover letter should be written so as to entice the employer into reading your resume, but that's getting ahead of ourselves. While we will get into more details in future articles, look over your current resume and ask yourself these quick questions:

1. Does it clearly present my name and all of my contact information?
2. Does it explain what type of position and employment I am looking for? (example: full time design engineer position)
3. Is my experience and expertise presented in the best light possible?

4. Does every single line/word on work toward the goal of convincing the employer to give me an interview? (If not, then question why it is on there)
5. Is my resume over one page? (Generally, most people should stick to one page)

Remember, your resume shouldn't tell the story of your entire career, just enough of it to land you an interview. Don't give up, keep working at it and you will find the position you're looking for.

Dan and Mike are providers of free, tested, and genuine advice given at http://resume-layout.blogspot.com/

Air Traffic Controller CVs - How to Write Them Effectively

During the recruitment process employers merely scan CVs, usually for under a minute, the average being 30 seconds. You should therefore ensure your air traffic controller CV is written in the manner employers expect. This includes attractive presentation, brevity, conventional use of font styles and font sizes. Above all, you will need to include only information that is relevant to an air traffic controller's daily operational duties.

Your air traffic controller resume should be written in 2 pages. This should be enough to fully highlight your professional experience, qualifications and training. However, if you are a supervisor or have amassed many years of experience within a Senior Controller position, your career profile might require more than 2 pages to fully highlight your expertise and experience. This is acceptable if you highlight only relevant information.

It is important to prepare your air traffic controller CV without clutter. The presentation and layout should be kept simple and easy for the reader to discern. Your resume should be written in black and you should also ensure it is consistent throughout the length of the document in terms of font style and font size. Times Roman and Arial are acceptable widely used font styles. Your CV should be headed boldly with your name using font style 14 or 16. The body of your resume should be written using font size 10 or 12.

The first few sentences in your CV will either encourage or discourage the reader. This first section is your professional profile and is your opportunity to briefly present your background as an air traffic controller and state your career objectives within this field. Keep your professional profile concise using 3 or 4 sentences. Following your professional profile, highlight your relevant skills in a bulleted key skills summary and keep the list to a maximum of 8 lines. Your key skills should include relevant skills such as the following:

* Ability to work proactively within a team setting
* Highly developed spatial awareness
* Ability to synthesize high volume of information from various sources quickly and accurately
* Excellent mathematical skills
* Good communication skills for issuing unambiguous instructions
* Ability to resolve problems and take decisions independently
* Ability to work in a calm manner under pressurised conditions including emergencies

If you are a newly qualified air traffic controller with little previous experience, you should highlight your education and training before any work experience, ensuring that you highlight relevant accreditations and other qualifications in subjects such as English and Mathematics. If you are an experienced air traffic controller then you should present your professional work experience before your education and training. Your work experience should, describe how you use relevant skills in your daily duties and where possible, how you were able to further develop these skills and acquire new relevant skills.

Finally, always write your CV in the third person and keep use of "I" to a minimum. Also ensure you consistently use dates along with names of educational institutions attended and names of employers. Employers also like to see records of achievement and other significant results such as commendable actions under emergency situations. These should be highlighted at the top of your CV.

Richard Blake is a senior CV consultant providing an online Professional CV Writing Service <http://www.professional-cv-writingservices.co.uk> catering for school leavers, graduates, and professionals up to senior executives and CEOs. Services also include airline pilot CV <http://www.professional-cv-writingservices.co.uk/cvs/airline-pilot-cv.html> preparation along with cover letters.

How to Write a Winning Cover Letter and Land Your Dream Job

Knowing how to write a winning cover letter takes you a big step further towards your dream job. After all, it is what convinces your potential employer to look into your resume, and try to find out more information, that would help them decide whether to hire you or not.

This task may seem rather challenging, but it's really very simple. Here's how you can get the job you desire.

Establishing A Goal

Before you become too consumed about how to write a winning cover letter, you need to understand this is your opportunity to introduce yourself to the company. Selling yourself comes shortly after; so you must not be too aggressive, but you also need to be affirmative.

The objective or goal for writing a cover letter is already determined. However, the idea of establishing a goal here is to be able to persuade your potential employer such that they will realize your potential to help the company succeed.

What part of your resume do you want to highlight? Make sure that you provide a glimpse of that in your cover letter, so your recruiters will have a decent idea on what you can offer.

Even if you have an impressive resume, if you cannot let that show through your cover letter, they will not be convinced to let you proceed onto the next phase of the application.

Important Elements Of A Cover Letter

One of the vital factors on how to write a winning cover letter for a certain job posting is to do research about the company you are applying for. Therefore, you become aware of the company's needs.

Most employers nowadays look closely at skills and what each employee can offer the company. Therefore, you can tailor your cover letter to appeal to the company's needs and this will enable you to stand out from other applicants.

Make sure to make reference to your resume in your cover letter. This is crucial when you have an impressive resume, since it creates awareness of your previous educational or job accomplishments.

When writing your cover letter, you need to address your employer properly by using a professional salutation.

Mention where you saw the job posting on your cover letter as well. Then slightly discuss how your skills are able to match the job requirements, and what else you can offer the company for that particular job position.

Knowing how to write a winning cover letter doesn't take rocket science. As long as you have the desire and skills for the job, you can attain your dream career.

Want to get your dream job? Discover how to write a cover letter <http://www.squidoo.com/how-to-write-a-cover-letter-for-a-resume> that grabs attention like a magnet, and secrets of preparing for a job interview <http://www.20daypersuasion.com/job-interview.htm> that gets you hired on the spot!

Writing Business and Cover Letters

The knowledge of how to write a formal business letter is an important skill. It is equally important to know how to write a cover letter. People often unintentionally make mistakes that make business letters or cover letters seem less professional. The professionalism of correspondence between companies is very important. A business letter should never be written in a conversational tone, but should always be formal. To learn the how to write a formal business letter read on.

Typically formal letters, like these, are written in block format. This means that all sentences are left aligned or justified and contains a header. The letter will either be written on personalized letterhead or formatted to contain the appropriate information. If you must type this information start four lines below the header and enter your name. Below this enter your title. On the next line directly below insert your return address. Drop down three more lines and type the date. Skip two more lines and type the recipients' name with the proper prefix, title, and address on consecutive lines. Skip three more lines and write your greeting. Remember to make this a formal greeting. After the greeting you will begin the body of your paragraph.

The introduction or first paragraph should explain who you are and how you know the letters recipient if they do not already know you. Between paragraphs you should leave two lines. Next you should discuss your reason for writing. Always thank the recipient for their time and try to keep your letter as short as possible. After the body, be sure to close your letter professionally.

The closing of your letter is your final chance to make a good impression. Show that you know how to write a formal business letter. Employ this tool just as you did the proper heading and body format. Be sure to close in a way that is memorable, but not obnoxious. A simple, but good closing is 'Sincerely'. After this leave four lines and then type your name. In the space between the closing and your typed name it is important that you hand sign you signature. This personalizes the letter without making it informal.

When you are writing a business letter, think classy not flashy. Introduce yourself, be brief and to the point, and close the letter in a polite, but business like manner.

Sturat enjoys writing articles on topics like formal business letter <http://www.iqio.org/how-to-write-business-formal-letter> and how to write a cover letter <http://www.iqio.org/how-to-write-cover-letter> . For more information you can visit us.

Cover Letters For Job Applications - Why You Must Always Submit a Cover Letter

If you're considering whether you really need to to submit a cover letter with every job application you make, then this article was written for you.

Your job application needs to be a structured form created to gather detailed information regarding education, work experience and other pertinent data. There is little to no room to show the level of enthusiasm you have for the position or your knowledge of the business.

This is why submitting your cover letter with every job application you ever make is a good idea. By returning a completely filled out application with a well written, brief cover letter and you have distinguished yourself from the crowd in a way that most people won't bother with.

However, something to consider is that today many companies have crossed over the digital divide and are only accepting applications over the internet. This introduces new questions on how to effectively and properly submit a cover letter for your potential new job, and how to make sure that will be seen and read.

Submitting your letter via email calls for entering the position title in the subject line and what would have been in the body of the letter into the body of the email. Placing the text in the email body rather than attaching a separate letter improves your chances of having it read considerably - because it makes it much easier for the recipient.

Remember that the main point of your letter is to convey your level of interest and unique qualifications for the job being applied for, so take the time to create a good cover letter for each job application you submit. There are those that maintain that you don't need to send a letter with every application - and while it may not be required, it will certainly make a better impression. Providing a cover letter with your application adds a touch of savvy that could help and can not hurt in today's job market.

If you're looking for quality cover letters <http://www.coverletters.genuinefeedback.org> , you should take a look at my blog - where I'll show you the best resource available for creating an awesome cover letter in just a few minutes - Your phone will be ringing off the hook with job offers if you use these templates, guaranteed. Go here <http://www.coverletters.genuinefeedback.org> to go there now.

Cover Letter Format - Guidelines to Writing a Persuasive Cover Letter

Searching for an effective cover letter format? Then look no further. In this article, I'll reveal some excellent cover letter format guidelines that you can apply immediately in your job hunting pursuits.

A winning cover letter generally consist of three parts which amount up to three paragraphs.

In the first paragraph, you will detail why you are writing the company. This will provide context to your intentions for writing the company, which is to apply for a new job. Also, try to provide clues as to where you found out about the job posting and what got you interested in applying.

The second paragraph serves as the gist of your cover letter. Here is where you explain what you can offer and what skills matched the job requirement. If you have other skills or achievements, make sure to point them out by referring to your resume. Make sure you can convince them to read your resume.

The third and last paragraph provides means to follow up your application. You can slightly review what you have previously mentioned in the letter to provide more emphasis. You can also provide means for contacting you in case you are considered in the next phase of the application process.

More Cover Letter Format Guidelines:

1. Keep it brief and precise. Avoid exceeding one page.

2. Proofread your cover letter before submitting to ensure it is concise and written in a professional manner.

3. Check for grammar or typo errors.

4. Make sure you know what you are applying for so you can defend your claims in the cover letter during the interview.

5. Always end your letter professionally. As much as you try to learn how to write a winning cover letter, hiring managers also put a lot of weight on your level of professionalism.

Hope these cover letter format guidelines help you land your dream job. Best of luck to you and happy job hunting!

Want to get your dream job? Discover how to write a cover letter <http://www.squidoo.com/how-to-write-a-cover-letter-for-a-resume> that grabs attention like a magnet, and secrets of preparing for a job interview <http://www.20daypersuasion.com/job-interview.htm> that gets you hired on the spot!

Career Transitioner Resume

A career transitioner's resume is challenged with overcoming an undeniable obstacle: no related experience. Instead, it must rely on recent education to establish expertise. The career transitioner must learn how to expertly position transferable acquired skills. Here are a few tips to creating an effective resume for the career transitioner.

Strong Targeted Profile

Your profile, which is a condensed version of everything you offer the employer that is relevant to the new role, must be powerfully written to position you as a viable contender. Located at the beginning of a resume, the profile is the place to state your case for why you should be considered. For example:

Transitioning from over eight years as a Production Supervisor to Clerical:

What I offer your company:
- 2 years' experience as an office assistant
- Over 8 years of employment - never late, absent only 3 days
- Soon to complete Conestoga College Office Software Certificate; achieving 80% so far
- Recognized for exceptional work ethic, reliability, congeniality and commitment
- Verifiable workplace problem solving, taking initiative, and troubleshooting

Transitioning from Production Floor to Law Office Clerical:

Strong and articulate communicator with professional demeanour, graduating from Conestoga College with Law Clerk Certificate by end of December 2008. Additional studies in General Business and Human Resources (22 courses). Maintaining a 3.75 grade point average in part-time Law Clerk studies while working full-time and fulfilling family responsibilities. Motivated, organized, and focused, takes leadership role in class, and offers an aptitude for law.

Education

Relevant, and recent "state of the art" education belongs front and centre for a career transitioner. This section deserves appropriate emphasis, with possibly a listing of courses, a reference to a well-known instructor, marks achieved, awards conferred, inclusion on the Dean's list, or comments from Instructors/Professors. Insert a couple of relevant-to-the-job projects. For example:

Transitioner from factory manufacturing to law office clerical:

Law courses:
- Political Science
- Introduction to Law
- Litigation Procedures
- Mediation & Dispute Resolution
- Planning Law
- Municipal Law
- Ontario Municipal Board Advocacy
- Landlord and Tenant
- Small Claims Court
- Legal Research and Report Writing
- Prosecutions
- Job Shadowing
- Achieved "A" on essay in Mediation & Dispute Resolution course (working from existing legislation formulated opinion on citizen's rights being infringed upon).
- Committed to ongoing education: taking Corporate Law, Wills & Estates, and Litigation courses in the near future.

Highlighted Relevant Skills

A listing of relevant skills, gained either at past employment, through volunteering, or from recent education (which can certainly include self-directed learning) is not only appropriate, but gives the candidate a definite advantage. For example:

Transitioner to Clerical:

Office skills:
- Customer Service
- Administrative Support
- Prioritization
- Organization
- Time Management
- Office Equipment
- Computer proficiencies: Word, Excel, Office XP, keyboarding speed of 35+wpm
- Microsoft Office Suite, Photo-editing and updating Website

Chronological or Functional Resume

Neither option, in its pure form, is ideal for the transitioner. The reverse chronological does nothing to bring to the forefront the transferable skills, and the functional is often regarded with some suspicion by recruiters (who assume, right or wrong, that the applicant is hiding behind this format in order to obscure unflattering facts).

A highly effective format is the hybrid. Keep the chronological format and insert functional examples-relevant to the new field-under each position held. For example:

Transitioner from manufacturing to other:

Production Worker, ABC Company, Smalltown ON (1999-2008)
Reported to Production Supervisor as one of 20 production staff that produced 2,000 widgets hourly.

Team work:
- Added to productivity by becoming cross
- trained on all 5 job stations.

- Participated in weekly meetings
- provided ideas for improvement (3 are now in use), brainstormed solutions to ongoing issues (contributed 2 suggestions now in use).

Reliability:
- Recognized for perfect attendance with 5 Outstanding Attendance Award; other years attendance was amongst top 5% in plant of 800 employees.
- Earned reputation for almost 100% accurate work.

The candidate has highlighted two skills that are relevant to many positions. Others skills that fit this category might be Customer Service, Leadership Attributes, Relationship Building, Working Independently, Pro-Active Examples...and depending on the actual position, there may be transferable hard skills as well, although less likely for the career transitioner.

Focus your resume content on the needs of the job and you will position yourself as a viable candidate for an interview. Career transition success can be yours with strategy and preparation.

- by Stephanie Clark, New Leaf Resumes

Stephanie Clark, a respected leader on the resume scene, is owner of New Leaf Resumes. Recipient of an unprecedented three awards for outstanding resumes in the Career Professionals of Canada 2008 Awards of Excellence, Stephanie's cover letters are included in Joyce Lain Kennedy's most recent Cover Letters publication. Stephanie's clients, serious about managing their careers, appreciate working with a leading professional. Please visit her website at http://www.newleafresumes.ca for more information, or call 519-505-5627.

Stephanie Clark, BA, CRS, CIS, http://www.newleafresumes.ca. An Award-winning and published Resume Strategist, dedicated to advancing your career goals. Please visit my website for more information on the services offered at New Leaf Resumes.

Three Common Resume Mistakes That Are Easy to Fix!

As a recruiter for over 20 years, I have read THOUSANDS of resumes...perhaps even millions! Still, it surprises me that with all the help out there to write resumes, people still make these three common formatting mistakes.

Mistake #1 - Typos

Even with all the grammar and spell checking features, people still make typos.

Solution

I suggest you read your resume out loud, word for word. Really look at each sentence and word to make sure it is correct. You could also ask a trustworthy friend to look it over for you too and offer suggestions.

Mistake #2 - Using Personal Pronouns

Personal pronouns are words such as "I" or "we" or "my". A resume is intended to be a professional document written to represent a candidate - you! You don't want to come across as unprofessional or that you do not have good written communication skills.

Solution

Try taking out all the "I's" and "we's". Sometimes if you simply take them out, the sentence still makes sense. For example, "I sold more than 500 widgets per week" translates into "Sold over 500 widgets per week". This type of phrase works and is appropriate for your resume. Second, replace "my" with "the". For example, "my team was responsible for designing all the code for a website" becomes "the team was responsible for designing all the coe for a website". It sounds more professional when you phrase it this way.

Mistake #3 - Too many key words

I've seen resumes where they spend an entire page on keywords so that their resume comes up in every search done by a resume database or the internet. This is particularly true for technical resumes. However, it is very unprofessional and quite frankly, annoying. It doesn't truly represent what skills you have and can confuse future employers.

Solution

Go over all of your key words and pick the skills in which you are at least intermediate skill level. Select these as your top skills and make certain they are on your resume. If you don't have too many (say twenty or less) then go ahead and add the skills in which you are beginner or better. Unless you are a new college graduate, do not list skills that you have not used in your previous jobs.

Now you know what three common resume format mistakes are and how to fix them. Polish up your resume so that your skills, education and background stand out, NOT your unprofessionalism!

Claudia Loens is a Silicon Valley based Recruiter with over 20 years of experience. Now, she brings her expertise and insider secrets to the job seeker in her new book "Get Happily Employed Now" Learn how to apply modern techniques and the Law of

Attraction to find the perfect job at http://www.happilyemployednow.com Learn more about her job search coaching services at http://www.claudialoens.com

Online Resume - Let Online Technology Skyrocket Your Resume Exposure

The power of the Internet cannot be denied. But rather than describing all the benefits of the Internet (which you already know) let's get more specific and talk about how the Internet can be used to get your resume seen by people who need your skills and experience.

An online resume is different than a simple resume listing. Sure you can upload your resume to all kinds of resume websites. You know the ones . . . But does listing your resume on these sites really create the type of attention you need? It probably doesn't. In fact, playing around online emailing your resume, even to thousands of companies and employment agencies is not going to cut it. Why?

Everyone is already doing that!

To stand out in the crowd you need to get a little creative. An online resume that acts just like a real website can give you this creative edge to get exposure and to take control of your employment. Resumes are a dime a dozen. Most times your resume isn't even acknowledged no matter how well written. Sure, it helps to hire a really advanced resume writing firm. But eventually it all comes down to exposure. Networking plays a huge role, but most of us are not networking professionals.

A much better alternative is to market yourself online the same way a business would market their products and services online. You need to start thinking of yourself as a product or a service, or both. You are not looking for a job. You are marketing yourself. Companies who hire are searching for the best they can get. If you present yourself as someone looking for a job, you have little or no chance. But if you market yourself in a professional manner, you will soon find that companies will seek out YOU!

An online resume can handle all these areas. An online resume has all the advantages of any other business website. The key word is BUSINESS. Remember, you are not looking for a job you are marketing your skills and services just like any other business using an online resume. In fact, while it is still not too late you really ought to register a website domain name with your first and last name: www your name dot com. With your own domain name you can use your online resume for the rest of your life. And you can also market yourself for many other services or products besides your online resume for years and decades to come.

The Internet shares the wealth. It can also help you network in a way never possible before. For work reasons an online resume, and for other reasons you may not have thought about. The bottom line is this: It's a new world with huge opportunity and the best way to go about it is by looking at your Self in a new light. You are no longer a person looking for a job - you are a human being with a lifetime of skills and experience and perhaps even some talent. Market yourself accordingly.

Richard Woolsey is an Website Optimization <http://onlinetoday.ca> Expert Serving People and Business in Canada and the United States. As a Certified Internet Marketer, Richard Helps the Unemployed to Gain Employment Using a Professional Online Resume <http://onlinetoday.ca/online-resume.html> .

How to Make a Resume That Gets You Hired

There are a lot of people out there who are desperately in need of a job and they know how to make a resume. However the majority of people even though badly in need of a job tend to be lazy when making their resume. A resume is supposed to be a brochure that does a good job of selling your skills. If you resume is not properly designed you wont get a job.

Making a resume that sells your skills effectively requires time and research. You can't just download a resume template and fill in the blanks what you need to do is to draft out your own unique template. You don't need to jump to any conclusions and hire a professional resume writer. Even though you can but it shouldn't be the first option you jump to.

All you need to start drafting your own unique resume is a good word processing software. Microsoft office will do the job for you. You also need to make a list of all your skills and which skills you are really good at. Once you draft out the list of skills you then need to also make note of all the awards and certificates you might have received from your previous employer.

The first section you need to start working on is the objectives section of your resume. This needs to be interesting and to the point. Don't state why you need the job state what you can do for the employer and why they should hire you.

Your entire resume should reflect the fact that your employer needs you.You also need to focus on the skills you are really good at and sweep under the rug what you don't know. Focus on your strengths and your best abilities and you will have no problem bagging a job.

Get more help to make a resume <http://www.squidoo.com/how-to_make_a_resume> and make sure that you get that job! <http://www.squidoo.com/how-to_make_a_resume>

What to Say When Emailing a Resume

If you are applying for a position online there are some things you need to know before you visit the send button on your resume. This article is meant to help you avoid some of the pit falls that people make in emailing their resume.

First is introduce yourself and what position you are applying for. This does not have to be your life story just a simple introduction will be fine.Next you want to list briefly again if this is in an email the person has other things to do other than read about how you were named Employee of the Month five times at McBurger. By this point of the resume the person reading is probably leaning towards the trash or is still reading. Either way use words that will grab their attention.

If you are using a site like Monster then you will basically be able to build your resume and make it look professional with their online tools. If however you are going this all alone then you need to find out what format the employer wants the resume sent in. Most places use an plain text or ASCII format.

Write a brief overview as to any experience you have in the particular field you are applying for. In addition take the chance to market yourself to the employer. This is no time to be shy especially since the only thing to judge you by is an email. you are not there to make that first impression your email should do that for you.

The last piece of advice I have is to spell check your work thoroughly. again you are not there to explain any mistakes in your resume. After you write the resume run it through a spell checker. Then read it out loud to yourself and see how it sounds to you. After you have done all of that have a friend look over it and read it aloud to make sure nothing was missed. The last thing you want to do is make sure your resume is attached to the email and in the correct format> after all of this is done you are ready to hit the send button. If all has went right you will get a positive response back within a couple of days.

Get more help on how to make a resume <http://www.squidoo.com/how-to_make_a_resume> and make sure that your resume is perfect <http://www.squidoo.com/how-to_make_a_resume> for landing you your next job.

How to Write a Proper Resume in 8 Simple Steps

In today's economic times finding a good paying job is harder than ever before. That is why having a resume that will wow a potential employer over is more important than ever before. In this article I will reveal the eight steps to writing a resume that will get employers attention.

1. List all of your qualifications first and foremost. Detail all of your skills and qualifications in a clear and precise manner. Many people don't know this but most resumes are read by what is referred to as a "gatekeeper". This persons job is to eliminate all of the weak resumes. Make sure that when putting your skills you use keywords that will grab attention. Use words that are common for the type of job you are going for.

2. List your qualifications with experience you have with the job you are applying for first. If you are applying for a as a office manager then list any experience in that field first regardless of where it came in your work history.

3. Quantify your experience explain how much money your managing efforts saved the company.

4. Again use action words, this is where if the person looking over your resume will begin to make their mind up as to where your resume will wind up going. that is why it is crucial that you grab the persons attention.

5. Simply sell yourself to the employer. this is where you get to make a sales pitch as to why you should be hired over everyone else.

6. Keep the resume short yet being clear at the same time. You don't want to bore the employer to death yet you also don't want to leave them wondering as to what they just read.

7. Don't give any information that you don't have to again keep it short keep it clear. this is your resume not your life story.

8. Avoid simple spelling and grammar mistakes. Check, recheck and triple check for mistakes.

If you follow these simple tips you are not guaranteed a job but you increase your chances of getting that shot at it.

Get more help on how to write a proper resume <http://www.squidoo.com/how-to_make_a_resume> and boost your chance of getting that job <http://www.squidoo.com/how-to_make_a_resume> .

How to Prepare a Resume That Makes a Killer Impact

If you want to know how to prepare a resume for maximum impact then the first thing you should learn is sales. I know you are probably not a sales oriented person but in order to get the job of your dreams you need to be able to sell yourself effectively. Your resume is like a brochure of your career. A well designed and targeted resume can bag you an interview.

When applying for a job you are up against some trough competition so you need to be able to stand out. The first thing you need to do is to organize your content and format it in a readable and attractive way. You also need to provide information that is accurate and true i.e. your education, working experience etc. Your resume should get these points across your potential employer effectively.

If you don't have the time or don't want to go through the effort of making your own resume you can hire a professional. However professional resume writing services can be expensive. If you don't have a job there are an expense you might want to avoid.

Your resume needs to be as clear as possible. You need to clearly state what you can do but don't make what you can't do visible. The focus of your resume should be on your can do attitude and skill. Most employers will over look a few things you cant do just as long as you are eager to learn. This fact should be visible in your resume.

Once you have drafted out your resume with all your details and information you need to format your resume in the right manner. Don't just put in fancy fonts because that is not required. Just make sure that when you format everything is readable and clear when printed out.

To get more help on how to prepare a resume <http://www.squidoo.com/how-to_make_a_resume> check out these resume ideas <http://www.squidoo.com/how-to_make_a_resume> .

Cover Letter Help in a Nutshell

Cover letter help and advice is abound on the internet. Countless hours can be spent reading the different variations of the same information. It's easy to get "lost" in all this information. So here is what you need to know in a nutshell.

First of all, know the company and field you are applying for. This is the foundation to writing an effective cover letter. Your specific references to the company you are approaching for a job and correct use of the terminology of the trade will demonstrate both sincere interest and knowledge of the line of work.

Cover letters are not necessarily the first thing a prospective employer reads. Managers that handle thousands of employment requests a year may not read your letter first. Instead, your resume is reviewed first and your letter read after a determination is made on the job qualifications being met. The best way to create a killer package is to also make sure you have a well-written resume.

Smaller companies may read your letter first and make a decision from it on whether to review your resume. You need both your cover letter and resume to be sharp and focused on displaying the benefits of employing you.

Finally, it's a very wise decision to use the samples found on job application sites as a spring board to creating your own cover letter. The forms are easily spotted and reflect badly on your integrity and ability to produce original work. Make certain spelling and grammar is flawless. The quality you display in your cover letter gives the reader an indication of what they can expect from you as an employee.

If you're looking for quality cover letters <http://www.coverletters.genuinefeedback.org> , you should take a look at my blog - where I'll show you the best resource available for creating an awesome cover letter in just a few minutes - Your phone will be ringing off the hook with job offers if you use these templates, guaranteed. Go here <http://www.coverletters.genuinefeedback.org> to go there now.

Good Cover Letters - Tips For How to Write Killer Cover Letters Easily

If you want to learn the skills for writing a good cover letter, then this article will show you how.

Learning what I'm about to show you will allow you to write clear, focused cover letters designed to capture the attention of prospective employers. Remember that the average application gets 20 to 30 seconds of attention should impress upon you the need to write concise and efficient sentences.

The basic rules for how to write a killer cover letters that will help you to land that job are few. If applied consistantly, you will develop a knack for including detailed, intriguing information in the limited format of a cover letter - it just takes a little practice.

Writing a powerful job-getting letter boils down to writing perfectly spelled, grammatically correct, compelling statements containing information not given elsewhere.

Your letter need only be one page consisting of 3 to 4 paragraphs which contain the details of why you are applying to work for that company in the position being applied for, how your experience or knowledge fills the criteria they have given for the job, and how you will be following up on the submission of your resume.

Practice limiting the main paragraph of your cover letter to 25 words. It is considered best to only use 'Sincerely' as a closing for the cover letter and always follow up in the manner given in the letter.

Customize the letter with company names, job titles and your specific skill sets that match the job requirements. Don't forget to use the name of whomever referred you to them. Avoid the form letter tone by using details. This is the key to writing a good cover letter.

If you're looking for good cover letters <http://www.coverletters.genuinefeedback.org> , you should take a look at my blog - where I'll show you the best resource available for creating an awesome cover letter in just a few minutes - Your phone will be ringing off the hook with job offers if you use these templates, guaranteed. Go here <http://www.coverletters.genuinefeedback.org> to go there now.

Resume Misery - Are You Making Any of These 3 Deadly Resume Mistakes?

People rushing to write a resume, leave out important stuff and put in stuff not needed; in other words they "blow it."

Let's look at 3 of the deadliest resume writing mistakes job applicants make, and what to do instead.

Mistake No. 1 - Unexplained Employment Gaps - People show gaps in employment between, let's say, job three and job four, with no explanation. Others don't fill (explain) the gap until later in the resume. Too late. Your resume has been tossed or placed on the "big pile" never to be seen again. Pro recruiters check for gaps in employment first. Acid test to toss resumes fast.

What to do instead: Show explanation (going to school, raising children, caring for a sick family member, etc.) in same format as job listing. First line in caps show NAME OF COLLEGE, City, State. Show years only, no months, 2000-2003. Next line bold face upper and lower case: Pursuing BS degree in Accounting, minor in Finance. Next, insert brief description of part time work to "help defray school expenses." Gap filled.

Mistake No. 2 - Thinking someone will spend more than 11 seconds reading your resume - First time through, 11 seconds is average time spent with your resume. Less than 6 seconds at job fairs. You don't get a second chance to make good first impression with your resume, on line, by mail or by FAX. Recruiters each have stack of 200-plus trying to cut 97% of them. No lie.

What to do instead: Use two-page resume if you have had more than two jobs. Cramming your info on one page hurts you. Use two pages and lots of "white space." Use one inch margins all way around text. No type font smaller than 11pt. Plain black, no colors. Ivory classic-laid 24lb paper when you use hard copies.

Mistake No. 3 - Italics. Italics. Italics. - Huge mistake. Puzzling; some big outplacement firms use italics making your resume harder to read. Watch what happens when your italics-strewn resume gets faxed. Ugly. Who is watching out for you? No one!

What to do instead: Take control. Be militant. No italics. Select one type face and stick with it. No artwork or images unless you are applying for graphic arts job. Don't underline and don't use ruled lines. Use bold face upper and lower case for your job titles and caps light face for your places of employment. Italics are not your friends in/on a resume.

And now I'd like to invite you to claim Free Access to your own one hour (60 minute) one-on-one private recorded Job Search tele-conference when you visit http://www.resumesteve.com

You'll get 60-minutes plus Free to jump-start or re-start your job search and actually have fun doing it. Grill me and find out: No charge. No obligation. No spam. No sales pitch.

Stephen Q Shannon The Free Teleseminar Resume Guy

Free CV Help

As a professional recruiter and owner of a CV/resume writing business, I regularly come across great candidates all the time who wish they had asked or sought CV Help with their CV/resume before they submitted it to all those important jobs.

However, none of them think this help is free - how wrong could they be! They normally only learn this lesson once they have been rejected, and actually how much information and help is available to them for free.

The Statistics:

The statistics of the job search process are brutal. Most applicants learn form their mistakes, because getting to grips with the HR processes is too complex. But simple statistics can tell you much. In an average profile of applications to a typical job advert, whether that be via newsprint or the internet, the answers are:

- 20% of applicants are rejected because they don't include a Cover Letter
- 20% are rejected because they don't have the basic skills required
- 20% are rejected because of errors in their application - mostly spelling, also grammar

That last one is just a crazy statistic, and its one I always question when most good word processing programs include a spelling and grammar checker. But every month, my companies own statistics tell the same story!

So, how can candidates improve their chances of getting an interview

Free CV Help:

There are plenty of free resources to ensure that your CV is better presented:

- Microsoft: a majority of applicants will use MSWord to prepare their CV. So why not use the spell check, and the grammar check tools?
- Hewlett Packard: it is more difficult to see typing and grammatical errors in your CV on your PC screen. Once you are happy with a version of your CV, print it out
- A red pen: to ensure that the printed version is correct in both spelling (spell checkers ensure the words exist in English, not that they are the right words), and grammatically, scan it through using a red pen to lead your eye across the page. Mark any errors
- A highlighter pen: with a paper version of the job advert, use a highlighter to pick out the first five key skills/competencies. Now see if you can find the same five skills/competencies in your own CV. If you can't, you will be rejected
- Read it out loud: check that it reads well. To ensure this, stand up and read it out loud - this makes it easier to spot poor sentences
- Your eyes: Having printed out a now literally correct version of your CV, take each page and hold it out at arms length.

Does it look correct, is there a balance between the black ink and white paper?

Now you have a version of your CV which probably contains at least ten less mistakes, and hence ten less reasons for rejection. However, this is only your own check, so there are two more free resources you can use before sending your CV in for a job application. Ideally, you need to use these resources at least three times to ensure the best optimised CV version.

Firstly, many Professional CV writers provide free CV/resume reviews. These are often - like our own - are marketing driven services, but offer dedicated self-CV writers excellent and free access to professional resources. Secondly, there are also your friends. Ideally at least one could be a present or ex-HR professional, but make sure it is read by at least one man, and one woman - women are generally more detail orientated, but you never know who will be the first person to review your CV in the desired employer.

If candidates used this information and process to check their CV's and ensure they were optimised for free, they would significantly reduce their chances of rejection, and increase their possibility of interview.

Good Luck!

Ian R McAllister is the founder of Ajiri, a UK group focused recruitment and employment in skills-short professional sectors, presently covering IT, telecoms and project management. Ajiri also provides professional candidate information and services via a series of online resources, including The Professional CV <http://cv4.biz/> from CV4.biz <http://cv4.biz/>

How to Write an Effective Internship Cover Letter - Four Guidelines to Guarantee Success

Your internship cover letter is the most important letter of your career. It gets the attention of the hiring manager thereby getting you the interview, where your personality, passion, and educational experience get you the job. In other words, it gets your foot in the door. Once you have a successful internship under your belt, your career will flourish. However it's important to learn some simple guidelines before you start.

Here are five guidelines for writing the most effective internship cover letter.

Do Your Homework

? Know the name of the hiring manager and address your letter directly to him or her.

? Gather information about the organization's goals and internship program through online research and through speaking with former interns.

Introduce Yourself

? A cover letter is your first introduction to the hiring manager.

? Be polite, professional, and error free in your grammar and spelling.

Sell Yourself

? State your professional passions.

? Provide information about your relevant experience or education.

? Tie your passions, experience, and education to the goals of the organization and the internship position.

Ask For The Interview

? Ask for the opportunity to interview for the position.

? Provide your contact information, including phone number and email address.

? Let the hiring manager know you will be calling his or her office the next week to schedule the interview.

The cover letter is only the beginning. Next you'll have to prepare yourself for the interview. If you've done your homework, this should be a piece of cake; however there are some critical interview techniques that need to be perfected.

To learn the top 5 interview tips that will be sure to land you the perfect internship please read: Internship Interview Tips <http://www.easyinternshipguide.com/top-five-tips-for-preparing-on-your-internship-interview.php> today. This is an excellent article that will guarantee you success. http://www.easyinternshipguide.com is dedicated to helping people find a great internship that will launch a successful career.

Resume Success For Job Fairs

Here is an interesting observation to ponder, in fact, you might have thought about this already. Did you realize President Obama is having a difficult time finding the best candidate to hire for his cabinet? Is it possible his hiring criteria or formula is unrealistic? Or could it be that candidates aren't putting their best skills forward? More importantly, what does that mean to the average job seeker looking to get hired in the work place today?

I recently participated in a job fair where over 1500 job seekers showed up with their proverbial hat in their hand. Downsized, fired or looking ahead before the axe falls, these folks were all after the same result. Get hired, NOW.

I was there to critique resumes and make concrete suggestions to the job seeker they could implement to propel the hiring manager to rush to their phone and call them for an interview. Unfortunately, this was not the outcome.

I felt like I was in a never ending game of where's Waldo? I kept reading and searching for some phrase that would jump out and give me a hint as to what type of job they wanted. Sadly, the majority of the resumes I read looked more like an autobiography than a focused employment marketing tool.

I ended up giving the same advice to almost every person I spoke with that day. These basic tips will assist everyone in their search for the "phone call".

Keep it simple and to the point. As in, what is your hook? What have you done in your past that translates to what your new boss that you are the person to call? This is written as a job objective or a career summary. Use one or the other-not both. It can be as simple as: Successful Office Assistant able to multi-task, problem solver and rapport build with staff and customers.

Make it easy to read. If it needs to be decoded, you have lost your audience. Learn the verbiage of the industry and use it. Giving yourself a fancy title and multiple paragraphs on your job duties defeats your goal. If you sell the glue that binds book jackets say so. Describing how you customize specific adhesives to meet the formulary configurations of various materials just sounds silly, doesn't it? Your goal is to have the reader understand what it is that you do successfully. Unless you are a brain surgeon, what you do should be stated in simple terms.

Benefits sell; features won't in the resume world. In other words, a resume with your job description does not highlight what benefit you will bring to the company. Make your resume jump out to the reader. It can look like: Recognized for exceeding monthly sales goals, receiving Sales Person of the Month award Feb. - December 2008.

To the reader it means that you are successful in your current position and it's not a huge leap to think you will be successful with their company (if you are hired to do similar work).

Make spell check your bff (best friend forever). No kidding! The #1 sure fire way to have your resume go directly to the round file is having misspelled words, typos and incorrect homonyms on your resume. Have someone proofread before you hit the send button.

Take control of everything that is within your power. There are many variables that you have no control over when job hunting. What that means is perhaps they are really looking for a man instead of a woman. You might walk into the interview and look like an ex-girlfriend or boyfriend, and although no one would admit it, you get eliminated on a biased opinion. Face it, we are only human!

What we can control is which phone number we use. I suggest using your cell phone number. This is where you can be reached 24/7. You might consider a professional looking email address as well. Kickboxer001@yahoo.com or loves2shop@gmail.com is not the impression you want to advertise to your potential new employer. Email addresses are free. Get one with your name only and you will be surprised the amount of respect you will get.

And here is a bonus tip: If by chance you need to use two pages for your resume please do not staple it together. And, I know the world is trying to be greener, you need to use two separate pieces of paper to print out your resume. Front and back printing might be considered ecologically sound, unfortunately the only sound you will hear is that of your resume being tossed into the round file.

These are quick fixes you can implement on your own to get your resume placed in the "call pile". Remember, your #1 goal is to receive a phone call. Presenting a clear resume will ultimately move you one step closer to getting hired.

Sari Neudorf of SDN Consulting is certified as a Professional Resume Writer, Professional Employment Interview Consultant and Professional Behavioral Analysis.

http://www.sdnconsulting.biz

Writing a Resume Objective Statement

A resume is one of the most important tools that you can use in expediting your job search. It is the information that you would use to convince a hiring manager that you deserve an interview. It is not so much about your experience, but about how you word it that is important. Your resume is basically your personal advertisement to the employer to convince them they should hire you.

There are many parts and types of resumes. When you set out to put your resume together, you will need to research the type of resume that best fits your career history. Once you have chosen a resume type, you will need to gather all of your information.

The first part of your resume will include your contact information and name. The next portion of your resume will go one of two ways. You will either write an objective statement, or write a positioning statement. In years past, the objective was always the first part of the resume under the contact information. In recent years things have changed, and some experts recommend using a positioning statement instead.

What Is an Objective?

Simply put, an objective statement tells the employer what you are looking for in a job for which you would like to be hired.

Objective statements are controversial these days, because tight job markets give employers a lot of people from which to choose. A lot of employers would rather hear what you have to offer them rather than hearing what you want.

If you decide to go ahead and use an objective statement in your resume, then you need to understand a few basic points. State your objective sentence in a clear and concise manner. Use active verbs rather than passive verbs to describe your objective. Make sure that your objective is specific and does not use any generalities. If you say, "I would like an administrative job using my customer service abilities," that does not give the employer anything specific to evaluate you by. A better example goes something like this, "Executive level administrative professional with seven years experience in process improvement seeks to join a company facing the challenges of the new millennium head-on." This tells the employer exactly what your goal is and what type of job you are searching for.

What Is a Positioning Statement?

A positioning statement is similar to an objective, except that it focuses more on what you have to offer a potential employer. You will want to follow some of the same advice that goes with an objective. Use action words. This lends power and creates a feeling in the employer that you will be an achiever in the organization. Here is one example: "Diligent achiever, adept at collaborating with customer to produce quality content relevant to the end user." Notice the high powered action words, diligent and adept. These words will reinforce the idea that this applicant will produce positive results.

Whether you choose to use a resume objective <http://www.sampleresumeobjective.org> or a positioning statement, make sure that your resume stands out from the crowd. If you follow these recommendations, you are much more likely to get the job.

Jason Kay recommends downloading professional sample resume objective <http://www.sampleresumeobjective.org/> statements to help you write your own.

It's Your Resume Stupid - Part II!

When writing your resume keep these six principles in mind:

Purpose
Packaging
Positioning
Punch
Personalty
Professionalism

Purpose - You have to know what job you are looking for or trying to get. That's the purpose of your resume. If you don't know, then the person reading it doesn't either. It helps you write the Career Summary.

Packaging - Ask any Marketing Specialist about how important packaging affects the product they are selling. Yes, you are selling yourself! Does your resume look like everybody else's? The same paper, the same format, saying the same thing? Or, is it unique? You should use a high-quality paper, clear legible font that is easy to read, using a graphic if it's appropriate could be used or a company logo, distinguishes your resume from the rest. It has to look visually pleasing to the eye and also be reader friendly.

Positioning - This is how you format your resume. How you organize the information so your talent shows right up front. You have 15-20 seconds to make an impression. Don't assume an employer is going to take the time to read your entire resume. Your talent and value has to be spotted quickly, and that's upfront (Block, 2002).

Punch - Does your resume have punch to it? I read a lot of dull and boring resumes. Are you using the right action verbs that bring the most impact? Use them to communicate your skills, abilities, qualifications and credentials in a hard-hitting way. These action verbs should be chosen skillfully.

Personality - Your resume should mirror your personality. You can't be someone else. Not only that your real personality will show during the interview. If it's different than what's on your resume you got a problem and it will be picked up by the person that interviews you. Turn those boring statements on your resume to something more interesting and hard-hitting. For example; instead of saying top performer, say peak performer. Instead of saying responsible for, show that you were a catalyst for major improvements in...Instead of saying excellent skills, say polished interpersonal and rapport-building skills, a solid record of success with, tenacious, significantly enhance growth, profits and return on investment, accentuating customer service, dynamic even, Do you see how these words are more hard-hitting than excellent, outstanding, great, very good at? (Block, 2002).

Professionalism - When you prepare for an interview you make sure you have a professional appearance right? Well your resume should look and sound the same way. For some reason this has gone by the wayside because job seekers feel it's not noticed. believe me it is!

We use a model called "The Organizational Message Chart" when creating a resume, not a template. This model was created by Jay A. Block, and you can look it up on the internet. It's written with a company's organization chart in mind. At the top is what we call a "Presidential Message", a short message conveying the message of why an employer should hire you. Then everything beneath that support this message. I want to teach you this method. I am giving a free workshop in the NJ/NY area soon, and I

I will also facilitate a free Webinar about this subject. Shoot me an email if you want to be a part of this.

**The information on this topic was taken from a reference book; "101 Best Resumes To Sell Yourself", by Jay A. Block

Learn more about what I do visit my website at http://fairrecruitmentagency.com This way we can help you further on how to market yourself better in this aggressive work environment. We offer resume and cover letter writing services to job seekers, and resume workshops to organizations, communities, groups and associations.

Resumes - Secrets of the Career Summary - Is it Mandatory?

A Career Summary is not mandatory. However, there are times when it will give you a tremendous advantage over the competition.

THE TRUE PURPOSE OF YOUR CAREER SUMMARY

The purpose of this section is to make your key qualifications instantly recognizable, and stand out in the mind of employers. When you have Relevant, Obvious, Specific, and Exceptional qualifications sprinkled throughout your job history, the summary gives you an opportunity to collect them all into one place -- right at the top of your resume. Employers will find them faster, which is super important, and they will pack more punch because they will be seen as a collection, rather than a number of scattered, individual items.

WHAT HAPPENS IF YOU DON'T USE A CAREER SUMMARY

If you don't include this section, employers will base their decision to interview you almost entirely on your most recent experience. That's because the stuff at the top of the first page of your resume gets the most attention. If you have only worked at one job, the Career Summary is not needed, and may in fact be redundant and work against you.

IF YOU DECIDE TO USE A CAREER SUMMARY

The easiest and most powerful approach is to customize the summary for the position. Write and format the rest of your resume without a Career Summary, and leave a gap between your contact information and your job experience, about 1/3 of the page. When you come across a position that you want to apply for, fill the space with bullet points that match your experience with the job requirements.

For example, if they need:

1. 3 to 5 years of experience in accounting
2. Able to do administrative tasks
3. Must multi-task

You create bullet points like these:

* 3+ years of experience in accounting
* Adept at administrative tasks including: phones, calendar, meetings, coordinating events
* Multi-tasks strategic objectives with tactical issues

Ready to learn more about how to get more interviews <http://www.magneticresume.com> for each resume you send out?

Download my FREE 12-page report, "Anatomy of a Perfect Resume," at http://www.magneticresume.com so you can learn:

* The 4 most common deadly mistakes that people make and how to fix them!
* How to create the perfect Career Objective & Career Summary sections

* How to maximize your resume so you're the candidate your next boss wants to meet!

Scott Shane Holt has seen it all while hiring over 100 people, in good times and bad, and as an executive coach helping managers and other professionals accelerate their careers.

Three Things Your Resume Should Do in 15 Seconds

The staggering unemployment rate has turned the traditional job search into a struggle for mere survival. Among millions, the hunt for work mirrors a pursuit for prey through the overgrown weeds and foliage of a jungle. The obstacles are many, the competition is steep, and the time is short. Are you prepared for the challenge? Since the resume is usually the first line of contact between you and the employer, are you confident that it represents the best you have to offer? Does your resume speak volumes for you-in 15 seconds or less? In order to get your foot in the door, it better do just that!

With so few jobs, so many applicants and so little time, employers are hard pressed to find qualified candidates. There is no shortage of candidates, but are they qualified? Will they be a good fit for their company? How will hiring managers determine this?

Everyone knows that your resume is the representative speaking on your behalf when you are not there to speak for yourself. That's a pretty tough job for a piece of paper or two. But when that one resume has to compete with hundreds, maybe thousands, it is even more difficult for that resume to stand out and make your case. So what can you do?

Begin by putting yourself in the shoes of the hiring manager reviewing the mountain of resumes covering his or her desk! Most of the applicants are probably qualified. Most are no doubt educated. How will the choices be narrowed? How will the mountain be scaled back to a hill or a valley? It's a good chance that the person in charge of making this decision is under great pressure to choose wisely.

By viewing this from a new perspective, consider what you would be looking for if you had to sift through all of the paper auditions coming in each day. This is no "American Idol". There are no audience votes or cast of judges, just you! With that in mind, think about what information needs to be conveyed to you in the shortest amount of time.

Your resume should do three things in 15 seconds or less:

? It should capture the employer's attention right away.
? Quickly detail your qualifications as they relate to the position being offered.
? Persuade the employer that he or she needs to learn more about you.

Your resume should attract attention. That is not to say that it has to have a siren or flashing light attached, well maybe. But the best course of action is to stay away from plain white paper. Be a bit adventurous. Definitely look for higher quality resume stock that offers a variety of prints and colors. Stay away from colors that are too loud or bright, but certainly put a little time and effort into your choice. Create a business card and attach it to the resume. This can also get the employer's attention. Aren't you curious when you see a business card? Then what do you do? You read it! So will the employer!

Your resume should quickly detail your qualifications as they relate to the position being offered. One thing employers hate the most is having to review resumes and applications where candidates have no objective or focus; for position being sought all that is stated is "any" or "general". The first thing that tells an employer is that you have no passion or true concern for the job the employer is offering, you are just looking for a job. Well, that is a given. Many are looking for jobs, but you are looking to meet the needs of that employer. Right? Even though you say you will accept "any" position that is open, are you truly qualified for "any" position? Would you really accept "any" position? Probably not. So, be specific. Even if that means you have to create a new resume for each position you qualify for, outlining a new set of qualifications and skills that match it. Do it! Take the extra time to make a resume that is specific to each position that you are after. Make sure those qualifications are listed succinctly at the top of the resume. Use bullet points if possible. Keep it brief, to the point and clear. An employer will appreciate being able to see this information quickly.

Lastly, your resume should leave the employer wanting more. Don't outline everything you ever did from grade school! Certainly list critical information that paints the picture of your being the right candidate, however not every little detail is needed. (This also goes back to creating specific resumes for specific positions.) Provide just enough information to get the hiring manager interested. Omit unnecessary details that have no real bearing on whether or not you can successfully complete the duties of that specific position. He or she will then put your resume in the "call for an interview" pile. Once you are able to speak to the potential employer personally, feel free to offer a bit more detail. Take that opportunity to regale the interviewer with past experiences where you completed a project weeks before deadline, closed a deal earning millions, turned an irate customer into a friend for life, etc. But on the resume, keep it short and simple! Or kiss your chance at that job good bye!

By putting yourself in the shoes of the employer, you see what he or she sees. Would you hire you for that job? If not, chances are, he or she would not hire you either! With times this tough, there is no room for error. Want to learn more about making yourself marketable for a position? Consider utilizing a career coach. There are group coaching sessions for jobs and careers forming now. Consider joining a 4 week course and begin to stand out amongst the crowd. The problem won't be where to find a job, but how to decide which job to take from the offers that pour in!

Visit http://www.GoalsThatOpenDoors.com for details on group career coaching sessions. A free strategy planning session is available to learn more.

Goals that Open Doors is a life and career coaching service helping clients to focus on goals related to any area of interest in life, overcome obstacles and create an action plan to achieve what is most important to them. Each client receives a free consultation/strategy planning session. Individual and group coaching options are available. Sessions are conveniently conducted via teleconference. For more information and to sign up for a free coaching newsletter, please visit http://www.GoalsThatOpenDoors.com

How Do HR-Recruiters View and Vet CV's?

The first person in most HR departments and recruitment offices who touches your CV/resume will not be the recruiter in charge of recruiting for that job. In most offices - assuming they are not using a scanning system, which serves the same purpose - it will be either their assistant, normally called a researcher, or an officer junior. They will have been given a clear and precise brief to reject anyone who does not meet that jobs basic functional skills requirements. So that is what they search for, to create a pile of CV/resumes for the recruiter to review. This process will reduce the pile of applications by around 2/3rds in most cases.

The recruiter in charge of the job will judge you on the appearance of your CV/resume. If it lacks signs of originality and creative thinking - such as the use of an internet template - you may not get the interview even when you are the best candidate for the job. A basic check here is to hold your CV/resume at arms length, so you can't read the words - too much white, or too much black are both bad.

Most recruiters still at this point have piles of CV/resumes to evaluate and have limited time for the assessment. They normally scan through the stack and throw out anything that is not interesting enough. Only the short list gets a second look, and hence a complete read through. The whole process is based on the content, format, lay-out and originality. It is thus worth the effort to be original.

The four stages of selection can be summarized in the following way:

* First glance: if the office does not use a scanning system, then a researcher will fulfil the same basic purpose. The researcher will glance at the first page of each CV/resume and if it fulfils the basic skills requirements it will be kept. They won't look at the second page unless the basic skill requirements are met on page one - a scanning system will scan the whole CV/resume end up in the bin unless a full history of the candidate is required. The CV/resume must be three or less pages, and ideally two. CV/resumes without an introduction or quick summary of the candidate and the skills or relevant qualifications also get placed in the rubbish bin. Long descriptive paragraphs and sentences earmark the CV/resume for the bin - ideally, keep sentences at 12words or below. Poor formatting and grammar mistakes are also frowned upon. After the first glance there are usually only a third of the CV/resumes left
* Second glance: now the recruiter will take their first look at each remaining CV/resume to establish whether the applicants skills, qualifications, career history and motivation match the job requirements. The recruiter must be able to identify this from the first page of the CV/resume
* The in-depth look: the remaining CV/resumes are visually scanned and then matched with all the job description criteria. The applicants are no longer thrown out - these candidates could fulfil other jobs vacancies - but the best possible candidates are picked for this job
* Final examination: only at this stage that the recruiter examines the content from the rest of the CV/resume in

more detail. They are looking for those skills, signs of innovative thinking, leadership, trustworthiness, and specific achievements that make the candidate right for the specific job.

As the candidate, you must ensure that your CV/resume survives the elimination stages and still stands out enough to get the interview. Relevance and engagement within the first page is the assured route to the final pile, the rest of the content and layout determines whether you get a telephone call let alone the interview. To ensure your CV/resume reaches the final pile, make use of free CV/resume review services offered by CV Writing professionals.

Good Luck!

Ian R McAllister is the founder of Ajiri, a UK group focused recruitment and employment in skills-short professional sectors, presently covering IT, telecoms and project management. Ajiri also provides professional candidate information and services via a series of online resources, including The Professional CV <http://cv4.biz/> from CV4.biz <http://www.howtowriteacoverletter.info/>

Putting Your Resume Into Words - How to Verbally Pump Yourself Up in an Interview

Some people are writers. Others are talkers. When it comes down to the job search, everyone has to be able to do both... and well. You can buy a book or hire a resum頷 writer to get the written part of the application complete. But how do you get over the interview jitters and really come across as the polished professional that you are on the job?

For those people who are naturally inclined in sales, the interview isn't something to be feared. Everyone else hates the stress interviews cause, and are constantly worrying, "Will I say the right thing?"

Getting to the point in a highly stressful situation is actually more of a critical job skill than you realize. Practicing speaking can build your competency in this core area. As a frequent speaker myself, people are stunned to hear that not only was I a stutterer when I was a kid, but also that I am an extremely shy person. You wouldn't know it if you met me! Fortunately, thanks to the dedication of a family member, I was quickly entered into the world of speech and debate throughout my high school and college years.

Then I was off into my professional career, and I remember quite distinctly being at a conference listening to a riveting keynote speaker, who had no notes and was fully engaging the audience. Wow, I thought, wouldn't it be great to be able to carry something off like that!

Fast forward twenty years, and through progressively responsible experience in my employment lifetime, I have had to step up and provide sessions and leadership at conferences and workshops. This thrust my own public speaking into a suddenly new role. The pivotal moment was when I was on stage addressing 500 people at an awards banquet, and I realized that this was just about the same as a workshop. You have a message, and everyone is there to hear it.

The interview is the same thing. You have a message about yourself, and the prospective employer is interested enough in you that they called you in for an interview to hear it.

A great resource for finding the supportive proving ground in speaking is Toastmasters. I am not a member, but I know countless people who have joined, and reaped the benefits as a result. They've been able to focus on what they are saying, how they are saying it, and sense how the audience is receiving their message. Learning what kinds of words or phrases could provide subtle clues as to your state of mind in an interview can be very enlightening. Use of "ums" and "ahs" are hedgers, and can communicate that you are not confident about what you are talking about, or let the interviewer know that you are very nervous and not focused.

Toastmasters or other clubs that encourage members to develop their speaking skills are definitely a wise investment into your skill set. You never know when you might have to give an executive-level presentation, or need to pump yourself up in an interview. If you are relaxed and comfortable with the act of speaking in a highly scrutinized setting, you'll perform a lot better by staying locked in on the content that you are delivering.

For more information on Toastmasters, please visit their website at toastmasters.org - and gain a whole new skill set!

Dawn Rasmussen - CTP, CMP
President
Pathfinder Writing and Career Services
PO Box 20536
Portland OR 97294
503-539-3954 phone
503-408-4894 fax
http://pathfindercareers.com/

Advance your career with a professionally-written resume!

Proud member of the National Resume Writers Association

Does Your Cover Letter Introduce Your Resume?

Most don't! People often say the same thing on their Cover Letter they already said on their resume. Just as if they submitted

2 resumes. Don't make that mistake with yours. Your Cover Letter is an introduction to your resume. It should make the reader want to go further and read more about you based on how you presented yourself (Block, 2002).

So, it should compliment your resume, not be a mini-resume in itself. You want to address those points about yourself that you have in common with the hiring manager or organization. Do some research on the company and read the job description thoroughly to make sure you understand it. It's all about how you fit into the organization and what you can bring to the organization, not what you want. Most employers want to know what you can bring to them, not what you want from them.

Then, what you are going to do is jot down those things you have in common with the company and it's culture, and talk about how you fit. Why should they hire you? This is the 1st impression the employer will have of you. You need to impress them quickly. Be creative, breakup the format of it with different fonts, use bullets, columns even, making it look different than everybody else's. Compare in one column the qualifications of the job, and in the next column how you fit with your qualifications.

So, save some of those achievements for your Cover Letter. After all, they may not ever get to your resume.

Learn more about what I do visit my website at http://fairrecruitmentagency.com This way we can help you further on how to market yourself better in this aggressive work environment. We offer resume and cover letter writing services to job seekers, and resume workshops to organizations, communities, groups and associations.

Resume Sample of a College Professor

A resume sample of a college professor would is be germane to most job-seekers since it would not reflect their unique ability, training, education, and experience. Rather, the important elements in a professional educational resume should be examined. These elements include the look of a resume, its effectiveness, and the ease of extracting the important information.

Usually, we submit a resume in support of an application. The resume reflects who you are and how qualified you are to handle the job. Therefore, it should be a "professional" document. You would probably not hire a person who did not care enough about a position to properly edit their resume. A written document can be a reflection of your character. A poorly prepared resume reflects a lackadaisical attitude and a lack of professionalism. It indicates that you may not be able to rely on this person when it counts. When possible, you should have a resume professionally prepared to be certain that you are being presented as well as is possible.

The resume should be designed so that the most important information can be obtained with only a cursory scan. This is usually all the effort that your resume will initially receive. Only the most important information should be presented in your resume and it should be devoid of excessive verbiage. This makes it easier for the reader to obtain and remember the pertinent information.

Work experience that is not related to the educational field should be summarized. This shows depth and breadth in your subject area. However, it should not be the main thrust. Your teaching and training experience should be the focus of your resume. You should also be sure to indicate your educational achievements including all honors and awards you have received.

A teaching resume should be designed to reflect that you are well-established in your field and that you have the background and teaching experience that they may require. The purpose of the resume is to get your foot in the academic door. Thus, it is important that the resume be properly designed.

If you are serious about earning significant amounts of money as a part-time professor then check out:

http://www.adjunctteachingonline.com/ right now!

Dr. Howard Rubin holds a BS, 3 master's degrees, a Ph.D., and was an NIH Postdoctoral Fellow. For 20 years, he was an environmental scientist and then started teaching as an adjunct professor. Dr. Rubin continuously increased the number of colleges and then started to teach online. He was able to substantially increase his income each year until his income goals were achieved and has been able to maintain this income level for more than ten years. Over the years, Dr. Rubin has helped many people to start careers as adjunct professors. It is within your ability to make a 6-figure income a year as a part-time professor. Unfortunately, the road to success is filled with obstacles for those who don't know how its done. Frustration and ultimate failure is the hard reality for most who try to attain this income level as an adjunct professor. Fortunately, there is an easier way to achieve success. If you are serious about earning significant amounts of money as an adjunct then check out:

http://www.adjunctteachingonline.com/ right now!

How to Create a Resume - The Right Way

You may already have a resume but this does not necessarily mean it's going to do the best job for you. Obtaining just about any position requires having a resume. Most employers will not even consider an employee without a cv. While just about everyone has such a document of one type or other, those who are more likely to be seriously considered for a position usually have a resume that is exceptional.

Before you start writing your resume, it is important to consider your past work experience very carefully. You will want to consider the types of tasks you completed in these jobs and the skills you acquired during these jobs as well as the skills you already possessed. Starting the process this way is an excellent way to start writing your successful cv.

You should also be cognizant of the skills needed for the position you are seeking. You will likely find all of the answers you need in the job advertisement and this is a vital stop in learning how to create a resume.

This is because most job advertisements include information on the skills necessary for the position. This may includes skills which the employer considers to be critical as well as non-essential skills which are preferred. Once you have this information, you can really make sure your resume is written to show what a valuable asset you will be to the company.

After you start to feel confident about the type of information you will provide, it is time to consider how this information will be presented as it can be formatted in various ways. The only thing to really avoid is a resume format that is too difficult to scan easily. This usually happens when the format is too busy. One way to keep the design clean is to utilize page breaks between sections on the resume. The sections you should include may vary depending on your industry. The most common sections to include, in just about any industry, include objective, experience and education.

Cynthia Penfold gives advice on how to create a resume <http://www.howtocreatearesume.org/how-to-create-a-resume/how-to-create-a-resume-getting-it-right> at her how to make a resume <http://www.howtomakearesumeblog.com/how-to-create-a-resume/how-to-create-a-resume-tips-and-advice> Blog

Resume Advice - How to Write a Winning Objective Statement

Have you submitted your resume about ten trillion times and ... got no response? Are you sure you have top notch credentials, beyond reproach references, an impeccable work history, and even reasonable salary requirements? If so, your problem is not the content of the resume. It's your objective statement.

Simply put, you have less than ten seconds to impress anyone reading your resume. And that's in good times! Now, with an estimated 7.5% unemployment rate nationwide, it is vital to have the right tools, in the right place, at the precise time. There are no second chances. Those less than ten seconds from a year ago have been severely reduced to less than five seconds! With hundreds of resumes for each hiring manager to review, you need to maximize your chances for success.

What exactly is an objective statement? It is your personal 5 second marketing advertisement. It is your chance to state in a few simple sentences exactly what you are looking for in your next position. It is found right at the top of your resume, directly under your contact information.

You need to be as clear and as precise as possible. Don't make people guess at what you want to do! If the objective statement is not clear, it just shows you really have no idea what you want, or worse, you are willing to do just about anything to get a job.

A hiring manager typically looks for the objective statement right away. He knows that a well written statement will tell him immediately whether you are a viable candidate. For instance, if he has one opening for a customer service supervisor on the night shift, and your objective statement says you definitely must only work the night shift, he knows right away that you might be just what he's looking for, and will definitely go ahead and read through the rest of your resume. On the other hand, if your objective statement says you are no longer interested in customer service and you prefer to go back to tech support, so be it. Again, he knows it won't be a good match for either of you.

What is important for you to know is that you can't try to, and shouldn't want to, please everyone. Don't write generic statements hoping to gain the interest of many hiring managers. This does nothing but backfire on you.

A statements such as, "I am looking for a job where I can utilize my past experience and grow with the company" means absolutely nothing, and offers no insight into who you are or what you want. This statement could be made by a secretary, a web designer, an interior decorator, a magazine editor, or a nuclear physicist. If a manager gets this far on your resume it will be tossed, deleted, ignored, or even laughed at. You just wasted your time and blew your only chance to impress the one person who might have wanted to interview you.

A statement that explains exactly what you are hoping to find in your next position and company is absolutely invaluable as you persevere through the job hunting process. Let's say you are an account executive who happens to be tired of traveling 90% of the time. That's OK! If you are still interested in sales, you can tell managers right up front that you don't want to travel that much anymore. It would be something like this: "Having been an award winning account executive for the past eight years for the southeast territory, I now prefer a more office oriented position that would afford me the opportunity to increase your customer base without being on the road almost constantly." This is perfect acceptable and much appreciated by anyone reading your resume. When a manager sees this he will know right away whether he should call you or not.

If not, that's OK! You don't want to waste your time at an interview for a job you don't really want, right? If he really needs someone on the road all the time, there's no sense in going any further.

Here's an excellent example of someone who had such a useless objective statement that when she was called about an interview, she was upset because she would be interviewing for a job she didn't even want! A resume was received by a hiring manager of a large computer firm. The resume was two pages of admin position after admin position. Nice titles, great qualifications. The objective statement merely said, "I am looking to grow with a company." The hiring manager thought this was wonderful and had an opening working for a department manager. When he called to speak to the woman about this particular job, she all but screamed at him, "I don't want a secretary job again! I want to get into your marketing internship program!"

She broke every rule and did everything wrong! A useless objective statement is just as bad as none at all. She wasted her time, she wasted an opportunity to perhaps even get invited to join the program (she should have stated that in her objective statement!), and she wasted the time of the hiring manager. The sad part was she had the exact qualifications of someone they had intended to invite into their marketing internship program. All because of a useless objective statement!

Simple rules:

* 2 or 3 concise, to the point, sentences
* Don't be vague about anything
* Don't try to please everyone
* Have a friend read it. Does he know exactly what you want to do based only on your objective statement?

Marie Duffoo owns and operates Miami Writing Machine, a leading provider of quality writing services. For projects requiring writing, copyediting, proofing, ghostwriting, or web content, you can can contact her through http://miamiwritingmachine.books.officelive.com Fast turn-around, reasonable rates, exceptional results.

Follow her on Twitter: http://twitter.com/MiamiWriting

Free Cover Letter Samples - Secrets to Finding and Using Them

The Internet is filled with free cover letter samples. Just do a search and you'll find hundreds of them. However, the biggest mistake job-seekers make is copying a sample word-for-word and sending if off. Cover letters are your chance to sell yourself to the company you're applying to, so make sure you do it by customizing the sample with the secrets below.

Secret #1
When searching for free cover letter samples, many job-seekers will do an Internet search that is generic, such as "cover letter samples". However, the secret to finding a sample that fits with your occupation is to customize your search more by searching for the type of position you are applying for. For example, if you are in marketing you might try the search "marketing cover letter samples".

Secret #2
Once you find a sample that fits your occupation, you aren't done yet. You still need to customize it for the specific job you are seeking and for your skills. Open the first paragraph with a general statement about the job and how your skills make you a good fit. Be brief, as you can go into more detail in the body of the letter.

In the second and possibly third paragraphs, go into more detail about your skills and accomplishments. Relate them to the job by reviewing the job description and pulling out the relevant skills needed.

Secret #3
So now your cover letter is customized to your occupation, the position you're applying for and your skills. Think you're done? Not quite yet. To make yourself stand out from the other applicants, customize it with facts about the company to which you are applying.

For example, if the company is a leader in telecommunications, you could say things like "I'm excited about the possibility of working for a leading telecommunications provider such as XYZ company and look forward to hearing from you soon". The deeper the facts the better - look for things on the company's website such as branding/slogans and past successes that you can incorporate.

So as you see, free cover letter samples aren't always free of custom work. Make sure to customize your cover letter to stand out from the crowd and you'll land your dream job soon than you think.

Greg Quigley publishes Qcomnet.com, a business writing samples site that includes free cover letter samples <http://www.qcomnet.com/free_cover_letter_sample.htm> . Qcomnet.com also provides other types of writing samples in addition to its cover letter samples <http://www.qcomnet.com/free_cover_letter_sample.htm> , such as sponsorship letter samples and radio commercial scripts.

Is Your Cover Letter the Best it Could Be?

First of all let's review what a cover letter is. Cover letters are used to introduce yourself and your resume, while clearly stating your desire to apply for a job position in a new company or make yourself available for a job position within a company. It is the formal introduction that provides a brief explanation of your job field, experience, areas of expertise and relevant knowledge in relationship to the job being applied for.

So, do you know how to make it work for you? Here are 4 simple aspects you should know and use to be sure that those 15 seconds (an employer would normally give to your letter) make him want to call you for an interview:

1. Use a strong first sentence. Try to give up on that introduction you tend to use, where you actually don't say anything; you know, the "I'm applying for that job I saw on your website" sentence. Since you have limited time to make a point, start more specific; something like: "Three years of experience in the real estate field, with a considerable number of sales is what I could bring to your company."

2. Use specifics. By that I mean that you should highlight your relevant experience and highlight some of your accomplishments in a "bulleted" manner. It's not the right place to talk about all of your abilities - if you will get the job, they will be seen in time and appreciated, but now you only want to get the job so only refer to those related to the job description.

3. Use a different cover letter for each application. It's not right to use a standard cover letter and just send it. Even if the positions you are applying for are similar, the ad itself sounds different and if you analyze it a bit you can see what that employer values the most. Taking this into consideration and the job description he provides, use a relevant content, shaped on each employer's needs.

4. No typos! I can not highlight this enough. You stand no chance of getting hired if you provide a cover letter with typos. It's a sign of carelessness or haste and that, other than a really bad first impression, if thinking in perspective, it will probably make your employer think about a possible pattern that you could bring on the job and again it won't help your case since he's in the process of finding the best candidate (and be sure that this dramatically decreased your value). Easy fix: proofread.

Is Your Resume Riddled With Bullets?

I review hundreds of resum鑊s per month, thousands per year, and one of the main areas of formatting confusion has to do with use of bullets. I see resum頡 after resum頟 with nothing but bullet points.

And I can't fault job seekers on this one. Many of these re□ sum鑊s are written by certified professional resum頟 writers!

What gives?

It never fails that whenever someone speaks forth resum頡 advice, the context always seems to get lost somewhere in the execution. Someone, somewhere, who must have been in the know, said something like this: "Use bullet points in your resum頡 because they are a great way to add emphasis."

And thus bullets have been splaying ever since!

First and foremost, people love bullets. And for good reason. They keep things quick and easy and are nicer to peruse than lengthy paragraphs. Second, people feel that when something is bulleted, it makes the statement seem more important. It tells the reader that in fact: "Hey, notice this point!"

The problem, however, is that a document full of bullets looks unfortunately more like most PowerPoint presentations or training exercise than it does an inviting document to read. And the idea that each bullet has something interesting to see gets convoluted when you are met with two full pages of them. All of a sudden you are saying that everything is of equal importance on the page, so instead of standing out, it now all blends together.

So what is a job seeker or a resum頰 pro to do?

Make your bullet points count. Infuse short paragraphs saved for basic job descriptions (up to no ~5 lines in length) and then use your bullets to highlight your most important and pertinent accomplishments). I'm not sure you can put a limit on the amount of bullet points used per position, but 4 is a nice number to go by.

To give you a better visual of what I mean, look at the following two samples:

Sample 1

? Led 40-person team to devise and execute strategies to transform city operations and community satisfaction.
? Engaged residents and businesses through various mediums to identify and address needs.
? Planned and managed annual operating budget and expenditures.
? Directed citywide projects and improvement initiatives.
? Overhauled 26 outdated ordinances, infrastructure, development standards, and financial practices.
? Achieved significant reduction in risk and liability exposure related to OSHA violations, legal and zoning disputes, financial settlements, and procedural documentation.
? Revamped billing and collection processes to improve cash flow, which enabled execution of 10% tax cut and subsequent re-election in 2006.

How do you differentiate from the list above what stands out as the main accomplishments?

Now look at the next sample:

Sample 2

Led 40-person team to devise and execute strategies to transform city operations and community satisfaction. Engaged residents and businesses through various mediums to identify and address needs. Planned and managed annual operating budget and expenditures. Directed citywide projects and improvement initiatives.

Key Achievements:

? Overhauled 26 outdated ordinances, infrastructure, development standards, and financial practices.

? Achieved significant reduction in risk and liability exposure related to OSHA violations, legal and zoning disputes, financial settlements, and procedural documentation.

? Revamped billing and collection processes to improve cash flow, which enabled execution of 10% tax cut and subsequent re-election in 2006.

Now it is clear what the day-to-day focus was for this candidate and what were the main highlights.

I'm not sure where and when the paragraph started getting such a bad rap, but somewhere it started falling under the category of "bad" or "uninviting." In Sample 2, if you had more context that you wanted to add or just wanted to break up the text a bit, you could do a really amazing thing: Hit Enter!

See what I mean:

Sample 3

Led 40-person team to devise and execute strategies to transform city operations and community satisfaction. Engaged residents and businesses through various mediums to identify and address needs. Planned and managed annual operating budget and expenditures.

Directed citywide projects and improvement initiatives. Proposed recommendations to City Council for approval. Created and facilitated financial training programs to disseminate best practices and standard operating procedures.

Key Achievements:

? Overhauled 26 outdated ordinances, infrastructure, development standards, and financial practices.

? Achieved significant reduction in risk and liability exposure related to OSHA violations, legal and zoning disputes, financial settlements, and procedural documentation.

? Revamped billing and collection processes to improve cash flow, which enabled execution of 10% tax cut and subsequent re-election in 2006.

Is it still too much to read for your taste? We could certainly argue that. But at least the bullets mean something now. The document looks well organized and thought-out as opposed to just a laundry list of items.

So whatever you do, consider how you splay your bullets!

So who am I anyway? Why do I think my advice is so valuable?

My name is Stephen Van Vreede. My company is called No Stone Unturned, and I have spent 15 years on both sides of the corporate hiring experience.

The short story is that I have an MBA in Marketing from Villanova University and a dual B.S. degree in Finance & Logistics from the University of Maryland. I am a certified professional resum頜 writer (CPRW) and a member of the Professional Association of Resume Writers and Career Coaches (PARW/CC). As I mentioned, I paid my dues in the corporate world eventually running a large-scale call center for a major truck rental company, and I have spent the past 7 years with No Stone Unturned, assisting job seekers in achieving their goals.

In February 2009, I launched a new group job hunting networking site: NoddlePlace.com. It is absolutely FREE to join, and you have access to everything on the site. Come check it out at NoddlePlace <http://www.noddleplace.com> . You can also follow me on Twitter <http://www.twitter.com/noddleplace> .

How to Write Cover Letters That Impress

While your resume will need to speak for itself to encourage prospective employers in considering your for a post, a cover letter can get you at least one foot in the door. Done well, it will grab their attention, create a positive impression and provide an incentive to review your resume with enthusiastic fervor.

Keep it brief and clear. You're an applicant among a pool of hundreds, if not thousands. No one has the time to listen to your life story. Make sure your cover letter indicates the position your are applying for along with a pitch that presents, in brief, the three main reasons why you're the right person for the job.

First impressions last. The cover letter is your first chance to make an impression. Since your resume is largely an inventory of technical and on-the-job skills, you cover letter will probably be your only chance to highlight the most positive aspects of your personality that make you right for the job. Pick your best assets and use them to put your best foot forward.

Grab attention. If your cover letter is a generic cut-and-paste job from the web, rambles on needlessly or shows a lack of ability to express yourself clearly, will they really continue reading? As such, your cover letter needs to punctuate the very essence of why you're the person they should hire. Make them pay notice and they will stick around to learn more.

Error-free. It goes without saying, your cover letter should be free from overt grammatical errors and half-baked thoughts. Use a software for English writers that can point you in the right direction if you're unsure. Read it several times as well to make sure your presentation flows smoothly.

Watch how innovative Grammar Check Software <http://www.englishsoftware.org/> instantly can improve your CV, cut your writing time in half and make sure you won't fail getting the job because of a lousy cover letter. Read more <http://www.englishsoftware.org/articles/english-writing-software/how-to-write-cover-letters-that-impress/>

Making a Resume - Tips and Techniques

Your resume is the first think a prospective employer sees when you apply for a job. During the process of making your resume you should always be cognizant of this fact.

We will explain some of the elements you should keep in mind when making a resume.

One of the most important elements to keep in mind as you make your resume is the list of required skills the employer featured in the job advertisement. The prospective employer wrote the job advertisement specifically for the purpose of finding candidates who possess specific skills. Your resume should clearly showcase any of the required skills you possess. However, it should be noted that you should never falsify your resume to include these skills, if you do not truly possess them. By contrast though, your resume should be written to really showcase these skills. You should also think about how easy it is for prospective employers to read your resume.

It is no longer recommended to limit your resume to just one page. Making your resume too long though is a mistake. It is okay to have your resume be two or three pages long if you need this much room to showcase your experience. It is also a good idea to think about how your resume will be formatted. Resumes can be formatted in numerous styles. Resume styles that are preferred though are ones that are simple to read. Resumes may be difficult to read because they are not designed in a clean and simple way.

In conclusion, it is always a good idea to think about including something to make yourself jump out at the prospective employer. Including a piece of positive feedback from a previous employer can really accomplish this goal. This can replace the standard line of, References furnished upon request. Most employers know you can provide references but may be intrigued if they see a sample of what these references will say.

Cynthia Penfold discusses techniques for making a resume <http://www.making-a-resume.com> at her How To Make A Resume <http://www.howtomakearesumeblog.com/> Blog

Free Resume Maker - Tips For Success

Anyone who has tried to create their CV individually will tell you that it is not very straightforward. The whole job at hand may result in some sort of uncertainty, so this may mean a resume maker must come into play. There are certainly plenty of resume making software programs to choose from. You can go for one of the resume builders on job sites or you can go for an actual software program. Once you've made your choice, it is then time to learn what can be achieved with a resume builder.

As you get ready to use these tools, you must note that some of the products downloaded directly from the Internet are not of a good quality. Using these inferior programs will result in poor resumes with little chance of success. In some instances, you may be better off using the services of a professional or another recommended program.

With a resume builder, everything is simplified. You are required to input information that is required to fill certain blank space. Before you get started using the software, it is a good idea if you have all of your information ready. This means writing everything you need such as employment information, school, etc.

You should start with your personal information. It is here that you input your name, your address, and your telephone number. These should all be easy to read so that the prospective employer can contact you.

The free resume maker will then move on to the next section, which helps you identify your talents and skills. This is the section where you need to stick to relevant information so you can impress the reader. You let the employer know how you can benefit their company if they hire you. Make sure you tell about your job experience and accomplishments throughout your various jobs. These details will tell the prospective employer that you have the talents they need to do the job. All of the information should be easy to understand.

It is now time to move on to the personal objectives. This is the portion where you indicate what sort of experiences and hands-on skills you have. The goal here is to make your case as to why you are great for the position. Do not hesitate to include illustrations to make them better understand. For example, you can mention a fundraiser that you did and how well you did with it.

It is in this section that you indicate your present and past employers and how long you were there. Make sure you include contact details.

This section is followed by education. This is where you will mention all of the schools that you have attended from high school on, as well as contact details. After this, you will need to list any community activities, memberships, experience, military, or volunteer work. All of these are very important to the job, so don't forget them.

The free resume maker can be a great tool when you need to create a professional looking CV.

Cynthia Penfold reveals secrets for free resume maker <http://www.free-resume-maker.com/> at her How To Make A Resume <http://www.howtomakearesumeblog.com/> Blog

Resume Writing Service - Tips to Choose a Professional Resume Writer

A good resume gives you the platform to flaunt your skill and experience. The current scenario of the job market seems dark. There are very less job openings due to recession. There are thousands of competitors for one particular post where you can't afford to get your dream job with a " just another resume" in your hand. Your profile should stand out and make you noticeable. It should be professional enough to touch your employer's senses. In this hour of grief, many writing services will try to convince you to take their service but without a proper research you should never fall under their trap and waste your money.

Here are some smart tips to choose a professional resume writer

A good resume writing service handles all kinds of job preparations starting from cover letters, resumes and personal statements. They should be interactive enough to know your inner strengths and weaknesses. They should know about you properly before writing that job-winning resume. They should have toll free numbers to enhance your interaction between you and the writer.

It is also advisable check the profile of the service provider. A good resume writing service will always have a website. You can easily judge their work by reviewing their websites and blogs. You can also read the testimonials written by their clients and then decide whom to choose. Experience matters a lot; an experienced resume writer is a better option.

Personalized touch is very important to make it real. A professional writer will interact with you more to get your inner view. They will try to write according to your perspective in a more professional way.

Getting the right job in this economy may be difficult , you need be innovative & work out new income sources. Try the free trial for Google Cash & learn the secret for earning thousands of dollars per month online.

Resume Layout - Write an Impressive Resume to Get Your Dream Job

Resume layout is as important as the content of your resume. It need to be well formatted and well written. While chasing for your dream job, people usually forget to take care of some minute details, which can make a huge. It reflects your personality and also gives you a fair chance to project your identity.

With the economic slowdown, the world isn't creating many jobs now. The job market seems dull and unproductive. There are thousands of aspired candidate for one particular post. The scenario is tough now but you can easily get your dream job with some extra care. Make your resume as impressive as you can and make it conspicuous and beautiful.

Here are some tips to write an impressive resume to get your dream job

Formatting: It plays a very important role after you write your resume. It enhances the look and feel of your resume. So always remember to leave a comfortable margin on the sides, top and the bottom of the page. It will make your profile look clean and appropriate. Proper spacing is also very important after every section.

Headlines: Write regular headlines before starting each section. Make it simple and subtle and also choose fonts, which are easy to read, and looks nice.

Avoid unwanted information: Don't provide unnecessary information, which will make resume long and unorganized. Be specific at the mean time make it little trendy. It shouldn't be a regular one. It should capture the attention of a reader otherwise it's of no use.

Avoid colours : Unless you are applying for some graphic designing course, it is always advisable to keep the color tone black and white. A laser printer and a

Getting the right job in this economy may be difficult , you need be innovative & work out new income sources. Try the free trial for Google Cash & learn the secret for earning thousands of dollars per month online.

Go here --> Google Cash Free Trial <http://www.loanratemodifications.com>

President Obama has come up with Stimulus Package that will focus on providing assistance to low- and middle-income Americans, to check if you qualify for Government Grants

Go here --> Federal Grant Programs <http://www.loanratemodifications.com>

FREE Trials are for a limited time only, so get yours today.

Resume Cover Letter Samples - Invaluable Cover Letter Writing Tips

If you have decided to search for a new job, you need to be really smart in writing your cover letter for resume. Cover letter is an application attached with resume while applying for job . This is a great tool for your selection if written in a proper manner. Though it cannot be a duplicate copy of your resume but it has to be a brief summary of it.

There are number of job applications that come in everyday to the hiring managers. We all know that not all are selected, some resumes are not even read once. The cover note of the resume shows the entire personality of the individual and so it has to be eye catching material.

Below are some invaluable cover letter writing tips:

1. You do not have to repeat all the stuff that is written in your resume. Be brief in explanation and write to the point. It

should include that you have applied for this position and some key elements about supporting material.

2. There should not be a single mistake in your cover note. No grammatical errors and spelling mistakes should be there. This may seem to be a small thing but it creates a very wrong impression about your personality and style in the eyes of the reader.

3. A cover letter should always be printed and never hand written. You have to be very professional while sending a job application to the HR. Handwritten cover letters looks very raw and unprofessional. Use Microsoft word and type the letter. And also, print out should be neat and clean.

4. Do not use any fancy fonts and language when writing a cover NOTE. It has to be written on a plain white A4 sheet in business font like Arial etc. No colours should be used to add any kind of effect. Remember that you are writing the letter to apply for a job and not for sending it to any art exhibition. It has to have a total professional look.

5. Use bullets and points for explaining the key points in your cover letter and always address it to the HR.

Best Job Cover Letter - Tips to Write an Impressive Cover Letter For Your Dream Job

A best job cover letter is the one which gives an impressive effect of your personality to the HR manager. A cover letter should be written in such a way that it is readily acceptable and is different from all. You must have heard that it can get you your dream job that is very much true. It must be written in a way that it compliments your resume and it should not be a copy of your resume.

The job cover letter must explain include the 3 things mentioned below:

Your interest in joining the organization

Your best key points which makes you suitable for the post

Your knowledge about the position that you are applying for.

Here are some tips to write an impressive job cover letter for your dream job:

1. First most important thing is the starting paragraph. The first paragraph of the job letter has to be short and precise. It should not be very long and should be meaningful. It should have a strong introduction about yourself, your working criteria and how you thing you can benefit the organization.

2. The job cover letter should be written on a professional manner, but at the same time it should reflect the traces of originality. You should not use raw language while writing but do not even use high profile language. Using big words may sound interesting but it makes your letter as if it is a copied one and has no personal emotions attached.

3. You do not have to talk much about yourself by using 'I' all the time. Include your interest for the organization, industry and the position. Tell how you would be able to contribute best for the company and what your tactics are.

4. Do not write information which is already mentioned in your resume. Find out different ways to communicate the things. Repeating the same information in the job cover note would just bore the hiring manager.

5. Use bullets and points in your cover note. It makes it easy for the manager to go through the whole stuff and it also looks good.

Writing a Killer Resume - Don't Let a Poorly Written Resume Spoil Your Dream Job

Resume plays an important role in finding your dream job. A good resume elevates your skills and experiences and makes it recognized and appreciated while a poorly written resume can spoil your job search no matter how experienced and dedicated you are. A thoroughly professional profile is the need of the hour. Due to global recession people are frequently loosing their jobs. The job market is dull and the competition is very high.

There are thousands of applicants for a single post and in this scenario you can't afford to search for a job with a poorly written resume. Every minute detail is now important in order grab every opportunity.It can make you conspicuous and beautiful and give the employer an everlasting effect!

How to write a killer resume?

Make a Smart Impact: Start your profile with something, which will generate the reader's interest. Your objective should be focused and persuasive and use right words while writing. Write interesting and intellectual hobbies. Sometimes they may the reason for your selection or rejection.

Keep it simple and trendy: A regular resume is boring. Make your profile look beautiful while keeping it simple. Use the correct sequencing of sections and subtitles and use consistent headlines. Avoid providing unnecessary information, which will make your profile content long and unorganized. Always be specific and informative in your points.

Fonts: Resume layout is as important as the content of your profile Use readable fonts and adequate spacing between every section. Don't try to experiment with colors unless and until you are applying for a graphic designer's post. Keep the color theme as black and white. It is always advisable to use a laser printer and high quality paper for providing that killer touch to it!

Getting the right job in this economy may be difficult , you need be innovative & work out new income sources. Try the free trial for Google Cash & learn the secret for earning thousands of dollars per month online.

The Best CV Format

There are many different types of CV available so you may be confused as to which CV will best present your profile, skills, qualifications and work experience. Before just writing down the information, you should research the types or formats of Curriculum Vitae that will present you and your career information in the best possible way in order to achieve an effective CV - one that gets you chosen for interviews.

There are mainly six different CV formats: the Chronological CV, the Performance CV, the Functional CV, the Targeted CV, the Alternative CV and the Universal CV. There are other names and of similar variations of the same, such as the hybrid CV, the Comprehensive CV and the Brief CV.

The Chronological CV is one that lists your education, work history, experience, etc in reverse order of the events. This is the most used Curriculum Vitae; however, it may not be the best CV to use for your situation. If you have just graduated from college for example, you may not possess a list of job specific specialised training, work history, or professional experience. This may be the ideal type of CV for a person that has performed well in his or her career and has plenty of information to add in a chronological manner.

The Performance CV is similar to the chronological CV, you can however, add achievements with the information provided in chronological order such as awards and information of the school, company, and a person to contact. This format is great for those with job experience of which to display a company in their work history.

The Functional CV the focus is on your career functions - i.e. an expansion on your skills performed. This format is often used for individuals / managers that are seeking a position in a different field. This CV type is also good for those for trades or technical employees employed on various short term contracts.

The Targeted CV focuses on the vacancy that you desire within a company. With this CV type, you only list education and work history that is relevant to the specific job position. This format is used by people that have been employed in various fields, but wish to focus on one job area or specific job vacancy.

The Alternative CV is one that is often used for creative people and positions. An individual can be a more flamboyant and add more personality to their Curriculum Vitae. This type is used by people that want to focus and advertise themselves rather than their achievements.

The Universal CV can be a mix of all of the above. If you are confused about which CV to use this is the safest one to present to prospective employers. Choosing this format is usually the best way to get the attention you deserve if you are writing your own CV. This CV will display the pertinent information you need in order to be chosen for an interview.

Mike Kelley is a professional CV writer <http://www.cv-service.org/> that has expertise in writing a wide variety of CV's for all types of employment. For more information on Best CV Format you can visit http://www.cv-service.org

10 Tips to an Excellent Cover Letter

We can call a resum頡 a technical document. A technical document has no scope for errors. What you present in your resum頩 is correct data. For example let us say that you were born on the 22nd April 1986. That is a fact. That is data verifiable. It is exact. Similarly your education. Only one unique individual such as you has one hundred per cent verifiable data that ties in to you and your records whether they be your parents, your academic grades, sports accomplishments and or any other such.

On the other hand a cover letter while technically speaking may not be a 'technical' document comparable to the resum顥 that is under reference, it highlights your other skills that may not be finite. That is the reason why we need to be more careful in crafting a cover letter. All errors and mistakes in creating a cover letter straight away contribute to your failure in provoking the HR personnel sending you the call letter.

So let us go through the 10 most common cover letter mistakes and see how you can over come them. These tips come to you from my experience of having poured over thousands of cover letters and resum鸡s.

1. Career Objectives: The first thing you should be doing is to address your cover letter to the job you are applying for. The HR executive is not interested in how that particular position is going to help you progress in your life. S/he is more concerned about what you did, how you are helping the current employer or helped the previous employer. Your cover letter should reflect your genuine interest in the position that you are applying for. Ideally it should also be clear about how long you intend to be with the company should you be invited to join them. Consider the difference between these two real-life examples:

Wrong example: " Though my experience as a Sales Executive is gratifying I am looking at an administrative position in Purchase department to help hone my negotiation skills."

Right example: "This Sales executive position excites me and am sure I would be able to contribute significantly to the turnovers if I am given an opportunity. You may please consider my performance with my current position."

2. Wasted space: Ideally cover letters need not extend beyond four paragraphs. You would be wasting precious white space repeating the obvious - mentioning the position and how you came to know about it and why you are applying,especially when it appeared in the "situations vacant" column. Instead of that it would be better if you just mention the skill sets that you have and how you would be able to add value to the position that you are seeking. A lot of rhetoric would be out of the window and only what matters, in this example is, your people skills and your experience should be highlighted. Mentioning other things that are irrelevant to the current assignment that you are eying only weakens your cover letter.

Wrong example: " This is with reference to the "Situation vacant", advertisement that appeared in today's The Times, pg 4, for the position of a sales executive. I have graduated from the University of Midlands, majoring in Sales Management." The HR executive is aware that you have applied for this position. Besides you have already mentioned it in your resum鮠. It would be better if you stick to establishing your skill sets as a Sales person and how you helped your current employer reach the set goals.

3. Cover letter templates / forms: There are plenty of sites out there that have a template or a form letter in place. It is like walking into a store and picking up a shirt. A shirt has a collar, two sleeves, a pocket and buttons right across the front to hold it in place. Similar for any letter, you have an address, a subject, an opening paragraph, an introduction and elaborate on it in the next paragraph and then you have a closing. There ends the similarity. The fabric of the shirt is different. The shirt you pick up depends on the occasion you have in mind. So is with the cover letter. The position you seek is different. The employer is unique. So are their expectations from you. You need to tailor your cover letter exactly to the potential employer's needs. You do not pick up a unisex, fit-all shirt. Similarly you do not have a universal cover letter template or a form. Every job is unique. So is every employer . Your cover letter should make it abundantly clear to the HR your commitment and familiarity with the position that you are aspiring to get into. HR can identify a template or a form letter and throw it into the dust bin or move it to the recycle bin.

In a real life situation I had come across a template wherein the applicant had filled in the blanks with a pen. The worst case scenario is that - you are insulting the HR.

4. Do not beg: Never ever pour out your woes into your cover letter and beg for a job. You should always quantify your positive attitude and make a strong pitch about why you think you are more suitable for the position. You should in your cover letter sound more determined and not at all desperate. The HR person should find a lot of optimism and enthusiasm from you towards the position. On the other hand should you pour out your heart about how important this job is to you he or she may be turned off by your desperate plea for employment. However, a fine line often separates the two, so the best advice would be to follow your instincts.

Wrong example: In one of those cover letters there was this plea: " Look I have my mom in the hospital and I need to pay those bills. So please help me with this job." A classic shout from the roof tops," "I AM VERY BADLY IN NEED OF MONEY!"

5. Missing resum矙: Check. Once. Check again. Double check. See all the attachments are in place. You have also mentioned in your Post Script that you have enclosed your resum頯 . But you forgot to staple it. It is very easy to forget to attach file while sending your cover letter through email. This is a fatal mistake. That HR is not going to call you or mail and ask you to send the resum頯 again. Because there are plenty of others who did it right without committing that grave and fatal oversight.

6. Typing mistakes: You call them typos. It is very easy to make all those typographic errors. But it is also very easy for the HR to discard your cover letter especially when it is full of annoying typing mistakes. You are deliberately playing into his or her hands. You are helping them make a choice that is detrimental to your success.

Here are a few common technical mistakes to watch out for when proofreading your letter:

* Checking the spelling of the name of the employer and see that you have it right.

Check to get the correct spelling of the hiring individuals name.

Check the address, email, phone numbers again and again and make sure that you got them right.

* It is very easy to make the mistake of indicating the name of one organization on the envelope and an other, on the cover letter you are inserting into that envelope, especially when you are applying many at one go. Please proof read and spell check.

7. Corrections: Your cover letter should contain all the relevant information. In case you have forgotten for some reasons to include your contact detail or details like email or your phone number and such things, please do not try to over write or scribble again. My sincere advice to you would be to fill in those details and

print it out again. It is considered unprofessional if you try to scribble, fill in with hand or worse still, lazy. Please avoid using a post-it or sticking something to the cover letter. Do not use the correction fluid either. It is always better to retype it and print it again. But before you print it again, proof read it for mistakes and omissions and commissions.

8. Photographs: Until or unless you are specifically asked to send your photograph never volunteer it. They are in the serious business of hiring talent that would complement their own talent pool and not otherwise. So please avoid pinning, stapling or attaching your photographs to either the cover letter or the re□ sum鮠.

9. Signature: Last but not the least. I have come across any number of cover letters and resum鱴s that do not have the signature of the candidate that is applying for the job. You should append your signature at the close of your cover letter and ideally the resum頴 too.

10. Stationary: Please avoid stationary that is gaudy and with bright colors. Never use your personal stationary that would send out a signal that you are too casual about your job application. White and ivory color papers are best with black print.

Your signature gives that personal touch to your application. So do it. Sign it before you mail it. Do not use a hand script font and spoil that sense personal touch. Sign it either in black or blue color ink.

Wish you the BEST OF LUCK!

Some more tips:

* You could use Arial or Times New Roman font - size 10 pt. Do not use transparent or personal stationary while applying.

* Let your cover letter adopt a serious and professional tone.

* Research the company you are planning to join. Try to have accurate details. Today there are many avenues that are open to you to find out much about these organizations. However while trying to incorporate such data in your cover letter make sure that it is accurate and authentic.

* 1667 Words

Anil Atluri
Web content provider
You can reach me at
the DOT achievers AT g DOT mail DOT com

Air Cabin Crew CVs - How to Write Them Effectively

Cabin crew positions are highly sought so it is very important to make sure your flight attendant CV is properly prepared. Employers rarely spend more than 30 seconds to scan CVs so you need to be aware of the skills and competencies airlines look for when recruiting cabin crew. These skills have to be prominently highlighted in your CV so that the reader can view them readily in a quick scan. Anything less will likely result in the resume being thrown in the bin. Your resume must catch the reader's attention and encourage him or her to continue reading. To achieve this, you will need to follow the following guidelines.

Your cabin crew CV should be kept to a maximum of 2 pages in length. This is readily achievable if you know what to include and what to omit. Your resume should include a profile, key skills summary, professional career summary and details of your qualifications and training.

Use only black ink and avoid clutter with a simple layout using font size of 10 or 12 for the main body of your resume. The document should be headed with your name in bold using font 14 or 16. One of the main features of good CV writing is consistency both in font style and font size. Use the same font size throughout the body of your CV and also adopt the same font style throughout. Times Roman, Arial and Verdana are acceptable and popular font styles.

Your flight attendant CV should begin with a short profile summarising your background, career and objective, all in a short paragraph no more than 3 or 4 sentences long. Your profile should end with your objective, focussing on your interest in working as a cabin crew attendant either as an entrant or as an experienced professional seeking career progression within the same field. Below your profile, you should highlight your key skills in the form of a bulleted list that bear relevance to a cabin crew position. Keep the list to a maximum of 8 lines. If you are entering a cabin crew post for the first time, then you should mention relevant transferable skills such as excellent customer service skills, good numeracy, fitness and ability to swim at least 25 metres. The key skills of a cabin crew member include the following:

* Ability to swim
* Good mental arithmetic for handling transactions
* Good communication and interpersonal skills
* Ability to handle difficult customers firmly and politely
* Ability to work effectively in a team
* Ability to stay composed and focused under pressure and during emergencies
* A confident and friendly personality
* Ability to work efficiently and quickly

If you are seeking a cabin crew position with no previous experience, coming straight from school or college, you should highlight your qualifications before any work experience, highlighting relevant achievements such as qualifications in English and Maths. If you are changing career to become a cabin crew attendant, highlight your work experience before your qualifications and mention use of relevant transferable skills in your previous remits. If you are already an experienced cabin crew professional, perhaps in a senior position, you should also highlight your work experience ahead of your qualifications and training. Importantly, avoid writing your work remit as a job description. Instead, use verbs to

explain what you did, mentioning skills used and how you honed those skills in the course of your work. Also mention other skills and training you acquired in the course of your work.

Ensure you write your cabin crew resume in the third person and keep use of "I" in your document to a minimum. Finally, always include dates along with names of employers and educational institutions you attended. Remember, a job application is a competitive process so always mention relevant information that will be to your advantage in the selection process, not least, your achievements and other significant results that are of direct relevance to a cabin crew job position.

Richard Blake is a senior CV consultant offering online professional CV service <http://www.professional-cv-writingservices.co.uk> catering for school leavers, graduates, and professionals up to senior executives and CEOs. Services also include cabin crew CV <http://www.professional-cv-writingservices.co.uk/cvs/airline-cabin-crew-cv.html> preparation along with cover letters.

Resumes - Secrets to Writing One Resume For All Types of Positions

In today's job search climate, it's pretty difficult to be interviewed based on a general resume.

The real question is why you want to have a single version of your resume. If I had to guess, I'd say that it's because resume writing can be a real challenge. Writing one is difficult enough. Writing more than one can be downright daunting. So you're probably hoping to write one version and be done with it.

REMEMBER, YOUR RESUME HAS A JOB TO DO

Your resume's job is to get you an interview. Period. It will do the job best when it contains qualifications that are Relevant, Obvious, Specific, and Exceptional, in the eyes of the employer. Along these lines, most job seekers customize their resume based on each type of job they are applying for; i.e. one version for project management, another for business development, and maybe a third version for grant writing.

The different versions will contain a lot of the same information. The job write-ups will be very similar, but perhaps with a few different accomplishments. The biggest changes will made in the Career Summary, where you can summarize the important information that you think will be most interesting to each hiring manager.

ONE RESUME, ALL JOBS

If you really only want to have one version of your resume, and you want to apply for several different types of positions, you need to network your way into your interviews. Friends, family, and colleagues will need to recommend you to hiring managers, and the hiring managers will interview you based on the strength of these recommendations. Once you get the interview, and it has been scheduled, you can give your resume the hiring manager.

USE A COVER LETTER

Another option is to have a single, comprehensive resume, and include a custom cover letter for each position that highlights the Relevant, Obvious, Specific, and Exceptional qualifications. The cover letter needs to bridge the gap between the specific job requirements and your general resume.

THE FASTEST, EASIEST, and PAINLESS WAY TO CUSTOMIZE YOUR RESUME

The easiest and most powerful approach is to customize the summary for the position. Write and format the rest of your resume without a Career Summary, and leave a gap between your contact information and your job experience, about 1/3 of the page. When you come across a position that you want to apply for, fill the space with bullet points that match your experience with the job requirements.

For example, if they need:

1. 3 to 5 years of experience
2. Knowledge of MS Office
3. Ability to multi-task

You create bullet points like these:

* 3+ years of experience
* Expert in MS Office Suite: Word, Excel, PowerPoint, and Outlook
* Multi-tasks strategic objectives with tactical issues

Ready to learn more about how to get more interviews <http://www.magneticresume.com> for each resume you send out?

Download my FREE 12-page report, "Anatomy of a Perfect Resume," at http://www.magneticresume.com so you can learn:

* The 4 most common deadly mistakes that people make and how to fix them!
* How to create the perfect Career Objective & Career Summary sections
* How to maximize your resume so you're the candidate your next boss wants to meet!

Scott Shane Holt has seen it all while hiring over 100 people, in good times and bad, and as an executive coach helping managers and other professionals accelerate their careers.

Resumes - Secrets to Landing the Job When Your Degree and Your Experience Don't Match

If you have a degree but you never used it, here's what to do:

REMEMBER, DATES ARE OPTIONAL

The easiest answer is to leave off the year that you graduated from your resume. This is a really common practice right now. Women, in particular, do this so that employers don't try to guess their age when they see that they graduated from college 20 years ago.

Write something like: MISSIE'S UNIVERSITY, BS in Computer Information

ARE YOUR SKILLS UP TO DATE?

Assuming that you remember everything that you learned in college, has the course curriculum changed significantly? Usually, you can check online for the school's course catalog. If you find significant gaps, or if you find new requirements mentioned in the job postings or during your networking, consider taking a course or two, to come up to speed.

If you find that college has become a distant memory, take a course, review your notes and projects, or do some serious self study to come back up to speed. If you ever wanted an MBA or a Masters Degree, and you have the financial resources available, now may be a good time to pursue it.

You can continue to apply for jobs, and the very fact that you are keeping your skills current will work in your favor.

The important thing is your ability to speak to the employer's needs. If you do decide that you need to take a course or two, focus on the topics that have come up the most during your search.

DO YOU HAVE ANY EXPERIENCE IN OTHER FIELDS?

Do you have professional experience in a different field? If so, then you'll want to include it in your resume, and then highlight your college-based qualifications in the summary section at the top of your resume.

Ready to learn more about how to get more interviews <http://www.magneticresume.com> for each resume you send out?

Download my FREE 12-page report, "Anatomy of a Perfect Resume," at http://www.magneticresume.com so you can learn:

* The 4 most common deadly mistakes that people make and how to fix them!
* How to create the perfect Career Objective & Career Summary sections
* How to maximize your resume so you're the candidate your next boss wants to meet!

Scott Shane Holt has seen it all while hiring over 100 people, in good times and bad, and as an executive coach helping managers and other professionals accelerate their careers.

Effective Internship Cover Letter - Write a Professional Cover Letter to Kick Start a Career

The effective internship cover letter will help you in winning appointment letter for your job. Be sure to attach resume with it and you will soon see your job hunting efforts start to payoff. It should be well written and creative which is a best way to make your resume attraction.

You are required to clearly state the company in which you're applying about your work passion and dedication for the internship. Showing a genuine interest in their company would definitely favor applicants who have enough knowledge about the company.

To write a professional cover note for internship, you need to follow these tips properly to kick start a career:

Firstly, keep your cover letter brief. Avoid those cover notes that are very lengthy and be sure to use clear and understandable language in it. A professional letter should not include any jargon, acronyms or anything which is very personal.

The first paragraph must be attractive enough which grabs the attention of the employer. Just keep in mind that he has to read thousands of letters in a day for job, so initial points must be powerful to qualify for it.

You are required to hire a proof reader which will help to check your cover note properly including spellings, grammar and overall readability. Remember the person you will hire must be a professional that will improve your chances of getting selected in the agency.

Send your letter to the right person and do not waste your time by contacting anyone who is not concerned with hiring for the job for which you have prepared a internship cover note.

Stick with one font in overall letter and avoid solid walls of text that will make the reader's eyes bounce over to the next cover letter. There should be lots of space in two words which will make easier for a person to read.

After sending your cover note and resume to the agency, make a call to the employer which will increase your chances of getting an interview.

Getting the right job in this economy may be difficult , you need be innovative & work out new income sources. Try the free trial for Google Cash & learn the secret for earning thousands of dollars per month online.

Go here --> Google Cash Free Trial <http://www.loanratemodifications.com>

President Obama has come up with Stimulus Package that will focus on providing assistance to low- and middle-income Americans, to check if you qualify for Government Grants

Go here --> Federal Grant Programs <http://www.loanratemodifications.com>

FREE Trials are for a limited time only, so get yours today.

A Customer Service Resume That Really Delivers the Goods

As a dedicated customer service professional, you need a resume that proves your industry expertise and showcases your skills to best advantage. Together with a focused cover letter, a customer service resume is a vital tool to get your job application noticed by the hiring manager and win you an interview.

Customer service is all about building and maintaining good relationships with clientele, with the aim of meeting their needs, providing solutions to their problems and creating an atmosphere conducive to making sales. But some accomplished sales people have difficulty applying those same skills to selling themselves -- which is fundamentally what you're doing when you apply for a job. Here are some ideas on how to write a customer service resume that will catch a recruiter's eye and get the opportunity to represent your strengths face to face in an interview.

Analyze the job advertisement or job description carefully and make sure that you understand the requirements of the position. Don't just scan the heading and job location -- you may miss valuable detail about the particular skills and roles sought by the employer. Extract key words and information from the description and make a note of them for later use.

Tailor your resume to the specific needs of the position that you're applying for. Don't just rely on using the same resume for every application you make. Take the opportunity to highlight those parts of your customer service experience that most accurate fit the needs of the employer, by crafting a skills summary and using bullet points to bring attention to key aspects of your background.

Show how you can add value by referring to what you have already accomplished. Don't just itemize the duties and responsibilities of previous jobs. Use what you have achieved to demonstrate the benefit you could bring to the prospective employer.

* Did you work in a call center? This can be a very demanding role requiring calm and professionalism while working under pressure, as well as technical skill in handling equipment such as multiple call phones.

* Do you have superior communication and organization skills? A confident and well-spoken telephone manner is desirable, along with the ability to manage a busy schedule of appointments and office duties.

* Did you foster positive relationships and develop your customer base? Providing satisfaction requires an understanding of your customer profile and sensitivity to their needs and aspirations. It also calls for skills of tact and diplomacy as you work to resolve conflicts and deal with complaints effectively. The ability to deal patiently but efficiently with an angry customer on the phone or face-to-face is a valuable asset.

* Are you experienced in the use of computer software? It may be necessary to manage a database of customer information, as well as using programs for word processing, spreadsheets, data entry and day-to-day communications.

It has often been said that the average resume gets about ten seconds attention before a decision is made about whether to screen it in or out. In order to compete in a tight job market, your customer service resume <http://1stclassresume.com/customer-service-resume-example.shtml> needs visual flair as well as compelling content. Check out this sample customer service resume <http://1stclassresume.com/sample-customer-service-resume.shtml> and find more helpful information about resume and cover letter writing and job interview technique.

The Resume - Your Work Experience

When an employer is looking at your resume, they are seeking answers to their questions. They want to know if what you have done in the past will meet the needs of their organization in the future. Everything in your resume needs to be evaluated with that in mind. Nothing should be put in your resume if it does not lead the employer to believe that you are the right person for the job.

When trying to decide what to put on your resume in the work experience section, ask yourself these questions:

* How do my skills compare with what the job specifications are?
* Will my experience translate well into the position I am seeking?
* Can this achievement help the employer see my worth as a job candidate?
* Does this responsibility reflect the quality of a good employee?

The idea is to highlight your skills and accomplishments so that they best fit with the job you are seeking. One thing that can be very helpful is injecting keywords that identify you as a confident, assertive worker. Using a word like "directed" is a lot different than "oversaw". Use strong, enthusiastic words to create a positive expectation in the mind of the employer.

Another thing to consider is that most job titles are specific to an industry. Unless you are targeting a job in your current industry, you need to make sure that your qualifications explain exactly what you did because your job title likely will not.

Mostly, just remember that what you put in the resume work experience section isn't supposed to look like a job description. It's designed to highlight your job qualifications in a way that excites the employer.

Carla Vaughan, Owner/Webmaster Professional-Job-Search.com

Carla is the owner of Professional-Job-Search.com <http://www.professional-job-search.com> , a web site devoted to assisting candidates in the job-search process. She holds a B.S. in Business from Southern Illinois University and has authored several books.

For more information about the job search documents you need to secure a great job, follow this link to: Job Search Documents <http://www.professional-job-search.com/job-search-documents.html>

Do Resumes Need to Include Months of Employment?

As a resume writer, I was always taught that resumes did not need to include months of employment, years alone were sufficient.

Nevertheless, recently, more and more companies and recruiters have begun demanding use of months claiming that by not using them, applicants are either "lying" or "hiding something." I spoke to a hiring manager recently who said, "I want to be aware of any possible gaps in employment."

This comment struck me as odd, so I questioned her some more on it. "OK, so you find out the candidate was out of work for two or three months in 2000. What does that do for you?"

Her answer: "I drop them from consideration."

I have to admit that I was stunned by that. As a former hiring manager, I cannot recall a time when I used a two-month gap in employment against someone, particularly someone who was otherwise qualified to work for me.

In fact, my thinking on that has always been, "but for the grace of God, go I." Who knows when that could have been me?

Let's face it. You could have numerous reasons for having employment gaps of less than a year. Health reasons, either because of you or a family member being one of them. Now who wants to put that on their resume "I was out of work because I had a major medical issue" or because "my spouse was sick."

So I responded to my hiring manager friend, "what if the candidate explained the job gap on the resume? For instance, they put something like "laid off from Jan. to Mar. 2000" or "medical sabbatical." Would that make a difference?"

Her answer: "Probably not."

My reply: "No wonder people lie on their resumes then."

In another scenario, I was having a conversation with a recruiter who was bemoaning the lack of months on most candidates' resumes. In this case, my recruiter friend made an interesting point: "If they leave off months, then a candidate can easily make one year look like two."

He then gave me a scenario:

XYZ Company: 2006-Present (but with months: Mar. 2006-Present)
ABC Company: 2004-2006 (but with months: Dec. 2004-Mar. 2006)
LMN Company: 2002-2004 (but with months: Jan. 2002-Nov. 2004)

His point was that if you look at the ABC Company listing, without the years, it looks like the candidate worked there 2 years when in fact it was only 16 months.

Again, my reply: "OK, so it was 16 months instead of 24. Otherwise, the client has had a steady work history. What difference does it make to the employer to know this? I mean, can't you find this all out when you ask the candidate to fill out a more extensive job application?"

His answer: "We want to know what people are hiding."

My reply: "I'm confused. What is this client hiding exactly?"

His answer: "Eight months of employment at ABC Company."

My reply: "So what difference does that make in evaluating this candidate to determine whether you want to interview him or her?"

It seems to me we have all forgotten the main intent of the resume: to review a candidate's background and decide whether you would like to move forward. After all, if a candidate is well qualified and seems to meet your needs but you are concerned about the actual dates of employment for some reason, isn't that something you could just...ask?

Maybe it is just me, but I am having a hard time understanding how the lack of months is the great differentiator. In the case of my recruiter's candidate, adding dates would not be a big deal. (Unless, of course, you see that "gap" from Nov. 2004 to Dec. 2004, and you just need to know how many days elapsed in there!). But in the previous case with my hiring manager, if a candidate showed a two-month gap, he or she wasn't even up for consideration! So what is a job seeker in this situation to do?

It seems reasonable to me that applicants should have some room for providing their background in the best light without being accused of "lying" or "hiding something." They should also not be stuck in a position where they feel they have to divulge personal information like an illness or family issue in the hopes that a hiring manager will be OK with that explanation.

I recognize that hiring managers/recruiters and the like are tired of uncovering lies later on in the process after a candidate is hired, but there has to be some room for middle ground.

So who am I anyway? Why do I think my advice is so valuable?

My name is Stephen Van Vreede. My company is called No Stone Unturned, and I have spent 15 years on both sides of the corporate hiring experience.

The short story is that I have an MBA in Marketing from Villanova University and a dual B.S. degree in Finance & Logistics from the University of Maryland. I am a certified professional resum領 writer (CPRW) and a member of the Professional Association of Resume Writers and Career Coaches (PARW/CC). As I mentioned, I paid my dues in the corporate world eventually running a large-scale call center for a major truck rental company, and I have spent the past 7 years with No Stone Unturned, assisting job seekers in achieving their goals.

In February 2009, I launched a new group job hunting networking site: NoddlePlace.com. It is absolutely FREE to join, and you have access to everything on the site. Come check it out at NoddlePlace <http://www.noddleplace.com> . You can also follow me on Twitter <http://www.twitter.com/noddleplace> .

The Great Cover Letter Debate

To cover letter or not to cover letter ... that seems to be the question these days. This past week alone on Twitter, my business partner and I must have come across or participated in no less than 30 discussions that started out something like this: "Do I really even need a cover letter? Does anyone read them anymore?"

At one point, someone even started a poll to gather opinions from around the blogosphere.

Responses to these pleas varied from "cover letters are worthless" to "one third of hiring managers say they still read them" to "social media is now replacing the cover letter."

Whatever your take, there is no doubt that the presentation of the cover letter is changing to suit the varying avenues out there for applying for positions. Some claim that a short e-mail (a couple paragraphs max.) is fine with your resume attached when sending the resume via e-mail. Others claim that the cover letter detracts from the resume and sounds too much like a marketing letter anyway so ditch it all together. Still others think you should direct employers to your blog as a way of "introducing" yourself.

For me, I think this discussion really misses the more important point, which is what is the purpose of the cover letter in the first place? And if you opt out of putting together a traditional cover letter, how are you making up for it elsewhere?

When you speak with hiring managers and recruiters, some of them will tell you that they do not read through cover letters because they all sound like stock form letters written for hundreds of people to read. Other hiring managers will tell you that they might glance at the first sentence or two, figure out whether the letter is pretty pointless, and then quickly move on to the resume.

If all that is true, then what that tells me is that the reason cover letters aren't often read isn't because they are antiquated or even unwanted necessarily; it is because they simply aren't effective and hiring people are tired of reading them.

Too often when job seekers are thinking about their resume and cover letter package, they are thinking about...themselves...and not about the audience they are trying to reach. This is a mistake for both documents, but it is particularly egregious when it comes to the cover letter.

Why?

Because a letter is a method of communication between you and the reader. If you aren't able to communicate effectively with your reader, then you aren't communicating.

Listen. A cover letter is your opportunity to showcase to a company what you know about it, be its culture, its needs, or its products/services. One of the biggest pet peeves that interviewers have is that they feel that most candidates don't even know, much less care, about the mission of the company they are applying to.

So take what you know about the company and line it up with your background and accomplishments. Tell them how you fit in! I heard about a candidate who actually made a two-column table and placed the company's job posting on the left side and then matched up those desired skills with his experience on the right side.

Personally, I like it when candidates talk about the products or services the company provides or quote from the vision statement of the company and personalize the letter that way. At least it says that you haven't just sent this same letter to 200 other companies. It says that you want to work with this particular company for a particular reason.

I know, I know. I can hear you now: "It's more time consuming this way." But is it really? Think about it. Sure, you may spend less time sending out pointless cover letters but more time on your job search overall. So why not take the opportunity to turn what is a missed opportunity for so many others into an effective tool for you? Even if it costs you a few extra minutes on the front end.

These days everyone is trying to stand out. Maybe the best way to do that is simply to do the basic things well.

So who am I anyway? Why do I think my advice is so valuable?

My name is Stephen Van Vreede. My company is called No Stone Unturned, and I have spent 15 years on both sides of the corporate hiring experience.

The short story is that I have an MBA in Marketing from Villanova University and a dual B.S. degree in Finance & Logistics from the University of Maryland. I am a certified professional resum頷 writer (CPRW) and a member of the Professional Association of Resume Writers and Career Coaches (PARW/CC). As I mentioned, I paid my dues in the corporate world eventually running a large-scale call center for a major truck rental company, and I have spent the past 7 years with No Stone Unturned, assisting job seekers in achieving their goals.

In February 2009, I launched a new group job hunting networking site: NoddlePlace.com. It is absolutely FREE to join, and you have access to everything on the site. Come check it out at NoddlePlace <http://www.noddleplace.com> . You can also follow me on Twitter <http://www.twitter.com/noddleplace> .

Tips to Design a Sample Cover Letter Or Resume For Software IT Professionals

If you are a Software or IT Professional, a lot if expected from you while you go on a job interview or send your resume via email to the HR manager. There are many things you should take care of while writing a cover letter. The design, wording, constituents or various components are very important to get noticed.

Cover Letter Writing Software is available online which you assist you in writing a professional cover letter for Any Job whether it is nursing, engineering, retail, software, networking or IT job anywhere worldwide. The Greatest Secret Tip to find a perfect software or networking job is to write a great convincing cover

cover letter or resume. You should use this every time you write one for you.

There are many things you need to consider:

Clearly mention your experience in various fields and various responsibilities at your previous jobs.

List the major projects you have completed or worked on.

List your major skills & expertise.

Various other things which need to be clearly mentioned.

Must Use the correct format and indentation.

You don't need to be an expert to use it. Even kids can make a manager's resume with that. The advantages of using a software are that you can get a professional cover letter in minutes. You just have to fill out certain details yourself and the letter is ready in a minute. Its very easy to use for everyone.

The software enables one to make an Attention-Pulling Resume Cover Letter while following the step by step instructions. The procedure consists of a only a few easy steps which one can follow from the beginning until the end. One just fills a few blanks during the steps. A TXT-file is created which one can save into a folder on PC or laptop. There are various important Expert Tips and tricks mentioned to enhance the probability of a response for a job interview. The software is focused on vacancies.

Check out Cover Letter Writing Software <http://latestexams.com/2009/01/how-to-create-an-amazing-cover-letter/> .

Download Cover Letter Software <http://latestexams.com/2009/01/how-to-create-an-amazing-cover-letter/> . It can help you design, write and print professional cover letters in minutes!

The Paperless CV - Maximise Its Impact

A paperless CV has many advantages over its traditional counterpart. Created and stored on a PC, it can be quickly and easily added to or amended, and sent instantly to any email address anywhere in the world. This gives you the opportunity to alter the emphasis if you wish to match particular job requirements, and know that you are not going to miss an application deadline. All in all a great improvement in the world of applying for jobs.

It has also opened up a whole new area for the jobseeker. You are now able to post your CV on the internet on sites that employers and agencies search when they require staff. Even when you are not actively looking for a job, therefore, they can still find you. It helps to amend the CV on a regular basis, even if only in a small way, so that it stays as a recent posting. Once it starts to age too much it can get lost amongst the many thousands of others and lose it's chance of getting you considered for a job.

So now that your CV's in a position where employers will come across it, how do you make sure they choose it for further consideration? They've got to see something that makes them want to read on, and hopefully then offer you an interview. I used to scroll through reams of CVs, and after a while it can get mind numbing. If you can make a difference to the person reading, it will increase your chance of getting an interview.

Some people ruin their chances straight away by use of poor spelling, punctuation or grammar. My personal bugbear is the incorrect use of apostrophes, which is guaranteed to ensure I don't interview you. A CV stored in electronic format can be checked for spelling and grammar automatically, so there's no excuse for getting it wrong.

The format of the CV makes a huge difference. It shouldn't be too long, should have current or most recent position first, and be more than just a list of past jobs. Remember, it has to stand out from the crowd.

There are plenty of companies who will review your CV free of charge, and suggest improvements. They will then revamp it for you if you want, but prices vary greatly so it pays to shop around. Having said that, an effective CV can be a useful tool for increasing your income so it's worth the effort.

One place to look is http://silicondiamond.com/page5.html who offer a free CV review, and an upgrade if you want it for only 27. One of the partners is an ex manager who is well used to reviewing CVs as part of the recruitment process. Now a partner in SiliconDiamond, he is using his experience to offer an affordable alternative to the many companies out there who offer a similar service.

http://silicondiamond.com/page5.html was founded to offer solutions at realistic prices, so have a look as part of your shopping around and see if it will work for you.

College Students' Guide to Writing a Resume With Little Or No Experience

You've served your time in college, putting all your efforts into school and only have a few internships or weekend jobs under your belt. As you approach all the pomp and circumstance of graduation, you panic, realizing that you don't have much to put down on a resume. What should you do?

Believe it or not, you do have enough to develop a resume. You will want to start this critical document by directly emphasizing your objective such as "A career in the field of Human Resources." This is especially important if you are targeting a specific career path.

Next, you will want to "show off" your degree to your prospective employer. If this is your first job out of school, your education section is an essential element and will be a decisive factor in the hiring selection process. Include your G.P.A. if it is worth bragging about.

The axis of your resume is the Work Experience section. Naturally, if you went straight from high school to college, you will have less work experience than others who went directly into the workforce. All hope is not lost. You may have to dig deep to draw out experience. Remember, it is the way that you present the information and the quality that counts, not the quantity that you present.

One strategy you can use is to stress your relevant skills and personality. For example, if you were a Peer Minister for your university, write how you developed relationships with the students in the resident halls. Is there a crisis you helped to solve while in that role? One student talked another out of committing suicide by using negotiation skills. The manner in which you show these accomplishments on your resume can present you as an efficient problem-solver.

How about that position performing clerical work in one of the college administrative offices? Did you use customer service skills that could benefit your prospective employer? If you worked with the soccer team, did you help to promote the groups' events by creating fliers etc.? What promotion techniques did you use? This would be relevant if you are applying for a marketing position.

Do not count out your summer work, internships, and volunteer experience at church or charities. Use a work sheet to take inventory of the skills you used in all these capacities. Even though unpaid, it is the experience that counts! You may be surprised to uncover the skills you have acquired mowing the lawn and working (entrepreneur/self-starter) or at fast-food restaurants (multitasking). Do not down-play your experience because you do not have a fancy title. The heart of your resum頫 is the skills you have acquired that can be transferred to subsequent jobs.

You should not make light of your outstanding academic background. Your ability to do well in school with a variety of courses show you can be a fast learner for the organization. Highlight your successes in the academic courses that relate to the job requirements you are applying for. Did you make the Deans List every year? Were you the commencement speaker? Make sure you mention these achievements as selling points on your resume.

Include an Honors section where you list any awards, memberships in honorary societies, and special awards. An Activities section should show your activity in various organizations or clubs during your time in college. Did you hold a leadership role? Including these roles show your prospective employment your involvement and dedication to these groups.

Show your enthusiasm in your cover letter. Usually, employers like the can do attitude that young people bring. While you want to sell yourself and appear confident, you don't want to exude arrogance. Emphasize your willingness to learn and go the extra mile.

Everyone deserves a chance to be hired. Think of the resume as a marketing tool and you as the product. Sell, Sell, Sell your skills. If you market well enough, someone will make the purchase. You may not start where you want to be but you don't have to stay where you started. Remain confident and upbeat. If you do not get a response from your resume, try and try and try again.

Master Resume-writer and Resume Strategist Claudia A. Samuels Newton is the President and CEO of Rewarding Resume Services (http://www.rewardingresumes.com). Claudia has a Masters of Management in Human Resource Management degree and a Bachelors of Science degree in Business Administration. With over 20 years of industry experience, she has served hundreds of satisfied clients. Her speaking engagements include being a featured guest on WLTX TV in Columbia, SC and serving as a resume-writing consultant for higher education institutions in her community. Samuels-Newton provides online instruction in Communications as an Adjunct Faculty member for the University of Phoenix Online. She also serves in a management role at Blue-Choice HealthPlan, a subsidiary of BlueCross BlueShield of SC.

What Counts in a Cover Letter

Writing a cover letter is a commonplace aspect of conducting any job search. When you apply for a job, even if the prospective employer does not ask you for one, it's good to send one as a way to give them a little more insight into who you are and what you're capable of.

But despite the fact that people write them everyday, many still are unclear about the more important aspects to keep in mind. So to help you out, let's look more specifically at what counts in a cover letter.

Using Good Use of Grammar

There's not much that stands out more in a cover letter than how it has been written. Yet, you'd be amazed by the number of individuals who send theirs out without having edited it - big mistake.

Remember, when sending a cover letter, writing is the only way to get your point across. This means this mode of communication needs to be perfect. Improper grammar usage or misspelled words can say a lot about how efficient an employee you are likely to be - at least in their eyes. So unfortunately, you may be an excellent employee who won't even be required to rely on written communication when working, but because of your cover letter being poorly written, you may not be called in for an interview.

Avoiding Fluff, Clich鳬s, and Generalities

It's a well-known fact that prospective employers don't have much time on their hands when reviewing cover letters. So it can be irritating when they're trying to read through yours to get a good sense of your skills as well as desire to work for them, and all they get in return is " ... and like my grandmother always says, you can't make anything of yourself unless you be yourself ..."

In other words, while it's nice to know that you listen to your grandmother's words of wisdom, it really doesn't have a place in your cover letter. And neither does showing how many big words you know or being too vague about why you're applying for the job. Your best bet when writing about yourself is to be specific about what skills you bring to the table (mention an example or two if possible). This way the employer doesn't have to dig through a bunch of fluff just to figure out why they should hire you.

Being Honest and Clear in Your Intentions

One aspect of writing that any prospective employer can respect is being honest and clear about the contributions you hope to make at their company. This means there is no room for template answers. Your cover letter should be tailored to their company, and honestly speak as to why you're applying and how you want to make a difference. Of course, doing so will require research on your part. But if you really want to be considered for the position then this is a step you should not overlook.

Writing your cover letter can be easy if you keep in mind what really counts. So dive in and write yours with care. Making a real effort to speak directly, clearly and honestly to a prospective employer will work wonders in getting you the call back you're hoping for.

Heather Eagar is a former professional resume writer and is passionate about providing working professionals with current, reliable and effective job search tools and information. Need a resume service <http://www.resumelines.com/> ? Compare the top companies in the industry at http://www.resumelines.com <http://www.resumelines.com/> .

What is a Cover Letter - Really?

Simply put, a cover letter is an introduction to your resume. It is the personalized document that accompanies the less personalized, bulleted form document that highlights your qualifications. Many employers request that applicants submit a cover letter. This becomes even more important further up the career ladder, as well as in positions that require excellent writing skills. The cover letter should not be mistaken for a rewrite of your resume in letter form. A less than presentable cover letter will lessen the chances of your resume being read. The following are helpful tips that should be used when developing your cover letter.

DO.....

? Address the letter to the correct person and make sure that names are spelled correctly. If you are responding to a blind ad in which the company or contact is not listed, then it is ok to put "To Whom It May Concern."

? Tailor your letter to show how you match up with the description of the job you are applying for.

? Include information you know about the position you are applying for and/or the company.

? Ensure that your letter is like a good novel in which the first few lines determine whether or not the reader will continue reading the book. You must GRAB THE READER'S ATTENTION!

? Include information that strongly supports information that you have stated in your resume.

? Reiterate how you will be of value to your potential employer. The key is to emphasize what you have to offer instead of what you require from the company.

? Be conversational and honest. Steer away from grand words and phrases that you would not usually use in a conversation. In other words, sound genuine. While you should not be too formal, you also do not want to sound too familiar. Use your creativity.

? Express your desire for the job and tie in your desire with your qualifications. Emphasize your most note-worthy relevant achievements and career successes.

? Let them know that you want to meet. Include contact information where you can be reached at to schedule an interview. It is not wise to use your current company's e-mail address or phone number.

? Use the same stationery that you used for your resume to show your style, balance, continuity, and coordination if using a hard copy

? Sign your letter.

? PROOFREAD YOUR LETTER. There should be no spelling errors. Remember the spell check feature on your computer will not pick up words that are correct but are used out of context. Have another set of eyes to read your letter. How embarrassing to submit a letter with your own name misspelled.

DON'T...

? Use a one size fit all letter for all the positions you will be applying for. Even if you have one cover letter, you must be able to make adjustments to tailor it to each position.

? Write monotonous run-on sentences that will bore the reader to death.

? Hand-write your cover letter. Make sure it is typed.

? Include personal information such as religion, race, marital status, or age.

? Include a picture unless the industry requires one.

? Sound desperate like you are begging for the job.

? Include information that does not pertain to the job such as videos or posters.

? Rewrite your resume

Job seekers sometimes wonder whether or not they need to use a cover letter at all. A cover letter should accompany each resume that you submit. Submitting a cover letter differentiates you from the other candidate who has not done so. It puts you in the unique position ahead of your competitor. Remember, the resume by itself does not convey your level of enthusiasm for the job. Your cover letter can create just the tone you need to make that homerun with the hiring manager.

Master Resume-writer and Resume Strategist Claudia A. Samuels Newton is the President and CEO of Rewarding Resume Services (http://www.rewardingresumes.com). Claudia has a Masters of Management in Human Resource Management degree and a Bachelors of Science degree in Business Administration. With over 20 years of industry experience, she has served hundreds of satisfied clients. Her speaking engagements include being a featured guest on WLTX TV in Columbia, SC and serving as a resume-writing consultant for higher education institutions in her community. Samuels-Newton provides online instruction in Communications as an Adjunct Faculty member for the University of Phoenix Online. She also serves in a management role at Blue-Choice HealthPlan, a subsidiary of BlueCross BlueShield of SC.

Resume Delivery Formats Explained

In your job search, you will read classified advertisements or Internet postings that require you to submit your resume in specific formats. Do not be alarmed. As the word format suggests, the contents of your resume will not change. The only thing that will change is the way in which your resume is presented.

Your presentation formatted (or fully-formatted) resume is aesthetic and appealing to the eye. It is usually created using word-processing software such as Microsoft Word. This format may include features such as bold, underline, italics, bullets, shading, columns, elaborate fonts, and even some drawing elements.

A scannable resume must be printed out on paper to a format that can be read easily when physically scanned into a computer database. The employer or recruiter will retrieve your scannable resume at a later time by entering keywords that are specific to the position they are seeking to fill. These keywords must be included in the top 80 words on your resume since some scanning programs only read the first part of the resume into the data base and save the rest as a graphic text to be pulled up later.

This scannable resume format is PLAIN, and lacks the formatting features of a presentation-formatted resume. Tabs are not used since it can cause different lines and information to run together, making your resume hard to retrieve from the database. Likewise, do not include parenthesis around phone numbers. It is good practice to send both a presentation and a scannable formatted resume when you are required to mail or fax your resume.

ASCII (pronounced Ask-ee) or Plain-text resume are generally used when an employer wants you to submit your resume in the body of an e-mail. It is also the format to use when asked to enter your resume on a form on an Internet resume database. In this case, you will copy and paste this version into the space provided. Some job websites now allow you to upload your presentation-formatted resume.

You will notice that this format of your resume is not as appealing to the eye as the other formats. However, you can change this by using some creativity such as making bullets using asterisks, capitalizing your headings, and using hyphens to border them. It is beneficial to use white spaces to achieve a look of a cleaner document.

Always copy and paste your ASCII resume into the body of an e-mail and send a test

e-mail message to yourself. When you open this e-mail, you will see what the recruiter will open on his or her end. Assess if this is the look you want to present even in plain text.

Things to Remember

Take care to follow resume submission requirements. Your prospective employer wants to know that you can follow simple instructions even if you have the credentials of the President of the United States. Also, do not send your resum頡 as an e-mail attachment unless you are specifically asked to do, so or your precious resum頭 may very well end up being deleted to trash.

Master Resume-writer and Resume Strategist Claudia A. Samuels Newton is the President and CEO of Rewarding Resume Services http://www.rewardingresumes.com. Claudia has a Masters of Management in Human Resource Management degree and a Bachelors of Science degree in Business Administration. With over 20 years of industry experience, she has served hundreds of satisfied clients. Her speaking engagements include being a featured guest on WLTX TV in Columbia, SC and serving as a resume-writing consultant for higher education institutions in her community. Samuels-Newton provides online instruction in Communications as an Adjunct Faculty member for the University of Phoenix Online. She also serves in a management role at BlueChoice HealthPlan, a subsidiary of BlueCross BlueShield of SC.

Why Have Multiple Resumes? Different Strokes - Alter Your Approach

The job search process can be a daunting journey that has to be customized in order to arrive at your desired destination. Tailoring ones approach is not foreign for any area in life. You've probably heard the saying, "different strokes for different folks." Let me go a step further to suggest for "different strokes, you must alter your approach!"

For, example, if you wanted to travel to Alaska, would you board a plane going solely to the Caribbean? How about packing beach gear to go enjoy the outdoors of that icy region? Unfortunately, your one size fit all resum頭 may not cut it as you travel on your job-search journey. Remember packaging a product can make a huge difference in how it is accepted. Rearranging your selling points and accomplishments may not be a bad idea as you venture out to obtain the job of your dreams.

If you have submitted the same resume to multiple companies and have not heard as much of a whisper back, you are probably guilty of the tactics used by the traveler visiting the Alaskan outdoors who packed for the sultry Caribbean weather. Using the same preparation to go to several unique destinations will only produce a fruitless job search. Unfortunately, developing one resume and blasting it to one hundred jobs spanning dozens of industries may not be the course you should be taking on your job-search journey. As a savvy job seeker, you must get into the minds of the recruiters and hiring managers who will review your resume to ensure you get the results you are looking for. What are the key words and qualifications that they want to see in your resume for that specific position? Use those buzz words. It will take much effort, but the results will be well worth your time.

Does this resum頭 meet the qualifications of the open position?

While it is not plausible for a top-rated chef with no PC skills to land a job as a computer programmer, a manager may be able to very well work in the human resources profession. Applicants can present their transferable skills in a manner that can make them marketable for multiple positions in a variety of industries. Why limit yourself if you have the key qualifications for the job? Think of the unique ingredients on your kitchen shelf that you can use to create a variety of succulent dishes. Your skills are like those ingredients, and should not be limited to one dish. It is your job to show the recruiter that you have what it takes to get that specific job done.

As the recruiter scans your resume, there is one major question in mind? Is this applicant qualified to fill this position? If you have the qualifications, but they are obscured in your current resume, it is your duty to make your skills visible so you can affirm that you are the perfect fit. You can accomplish this by designing a strong marketing tool that essentially forces the reviewer not to pin you down to a mere job title. This will greatly improve the probability of your resume being selected to pursue a face-to-face interview.

Researching to Craft the document

Sending the same resume may work for jobs that align perfectly with your background. However, there are other positions that will require you to tweak your document with facts not fiction and fluff. Even if you are qualified, you may not be able to sell your skills if you do not write your selling points as to create a match. This is called tailoring or customizing your resume.

Your first step will be to read the job description of your desired position several times to ensure you understand what they are looking for in the candidates. Next, make a detailed list of the experience, skills, and even education and training you have that fits that description. Again, you should not confine yourself to a past position title. While you worked as a sales agent, you may have developed valuable skills in customer service or even management. Who said you had to be a manager to have leadership skills? Likewise, the hiring manager is not interested in your certificate in real estate if you are applying for a job as an accountant. As a matter of fact, by listing irrelevant information, you may send the message that you are confused and elicit additional questions. Why are you in so many different careers? Are you unsure of what you want to do? How long will you stay with us before returning to your previous career? To avoid generating these questions, only list what is relevant. If there are irrelevant items in your Experience section, convert those into transferable skills.

By emphasizing your skills, you have ceased limiting yourself to a small pocket of jobs and shutting yourself out of a realm of possibilities. When you extract your skills acquired at your various positions, you have begun to unravel the fabric that make up your unique abilities that can be an asset to potential employers. This broadens your horizons. Along with those skills, you will need to show some examples of resulting achievements. Voila! You have taken the beginning steps to customize your resume to get the results you want.

Putting it all together - Is your objective clear?

Now that you have taken an inventory of your relevant skills, it is time to incorporate what you have uncovered into your existing resume. You should position your most relevant experience where it is easily noticeable. After all, the recruiter does not have time to read your document line by line to determine if you are a fit. Summarize your qualifications that are unique to the position in the Summary of Qualifications section to spark immediate interest.

Your job is to make the reviewer's job easier. If you are not trying to get in the restaurant business, put your waiter position that you performed at the local diner over 15 years ago at the end of your resume. More importantly, while you do not have to include an Objective section, make sure that your purpose for sending that resume is clearly understood as the reader scans it over.

What Resume Type?

Arrangement of the contents on resume is critical especially when you have unique situations. For example, do you have noticeable gaps in your resume that you don't want to stare the hiring manger in the face? Then you may want to steer clear from a chronological resume. Use a functional resume that highlights your knowledge, skills, and abilities instead of being position or title focused. By using this format, you will guide the resume reviewer to your high selling points. Your gaps may be for a legitimate reason and not because you are a job-hopper. Let the hiring manager and recruiters see what you want them to see. Of course, the information must all be true and you still have to be prepared to explain questionable items once you get the interview.

Before you submit your next resume, you must take the necessary measures to ensure you stand out. Alter your approach. Make sure your resume is tailored to each job you are applying for. By using careful strategy, you can get the coveted call for an interview once you hit the send button, the fax number keys, or licking that stamp before sending your resume in the mail.

Master Resume-writer and Resume Strategist Claudia A. Samuels Newton is the President and CEO of Rewarding Resume Services http://www.rewardingresumes.com Claudia has a Masters of Management in Human Resource Management degree and a Bachelors of Science degree in Business Administration. With over 20 years of industry experience, she has served hundreds of satisfied clients. Her speaking engagements include being a featured guest on WLTX TV in Columbia, SC and serving as a resume-writing consultant for higher education institutions in her community. Samuels-Newton provides online instruction in Communications as an Adjunct Faculty member for the University of Phoenix Online. She also serves in a management role at BlueChoice HealthPlan, a subsidiary of BlueCross BlueShield of SC.

If the Candidate Fits, The Hiring Manager Will Not Acquit

Have you ever read a job description and instantly lit up because it seemed as if they were describing you? The challenge is to get the person who will be reviewing your resum頴 to believe this as well. Applying for a job can be a very daunting task even when you know you are the perfect fit. Let's face it. There will be hundreds of qualified applicants who are just as educated and as experienced as you. How will you differentiate yourself from your competitors to command the recruiter's attention?

What Employers Want

Employers seeking to fill a position are on a mission. They are not in the habit of giving away jobs out of the kindness of their hearts. We sometimes hear that past performance is NOT indicative of future results. When it comes to resum頹 s, employers believe the opposite. Your first step then is to find out exactly what the employer is looking for in your past that will suit their current and future needs.

The Proof is in the Pudding

Develop a table with two columns. Label the first column, Job Requirements and the second column, My Qualifications. List each job requirement for the position to which you are applying, and develop a corresponding response in the Qualifications column. Never mind the mundane descriptions that other resum頹 s have. Most people claim to be a team-player, detail-oriented, and well-organized. These are "soft skills." Instead, give concrete evidence of why you can be described with these terms. Be sure to use impressive and relevant examples that can be verified. By the end of this exercise, you should be able to show that you are the solution to the employer's problem and a fit in the company's plan.

Establishing a Match Made in Heaven

Now is the time for you to tailor your resum纈 to match the job advertisement. Of course, you should not list the job description word for word on your resum鯱. Otherwise, your resum頜 will look like all those of everyone else. This is the time to brag about your accomplishments, not time to be shy. Show the relevant knowledge and skills that make you compatible for the position.

The chosen resum頹 s will be those of applicants who show how their current or past job positions align with the one they are applying for. Emphasize those positions that are similar to the desired job. Remember, the more emphasis you put on similarities, the more likely you will be seen as a match made in heaven. Your goal is to make sure your resum頩 is the perfect fit. If your resum頩 is the perfect fit, the recruiter will not acquit.

Master Resume-writer and Resume Strategist Claudia A. Samuels Newton is the President and CEO of Rewarding Resume Services (http://www.rewardingresumes.com). Claudia has a Masters of Management in Human Resource Management degree and a Bachelors of Science degree in Business Administration. With over 20 years of industry experience, she has served hundreds of satisfied clients. Her speaking engagements include being a featured guest on WLTX TV in Columbia, SC and serving as a resume-writing consultant for higher education institutions in her community. Samuels-Newton provides online instruction in Communications as an Adjunct Faculty member for the University of Phoenix Online. She also serves in a management role at BlueChoice HealthPlan, a subsidiary of BlueCross BlueShield of SC.

Resumes and Beyond

YOUR R□SUM□

While a resum頻 itself cannot land you a job, it is the key that opens the door to the interview. It is all the employers will know about you before they actually request to meet you in person. So as you can see, you must make a good impression on paper to land an interview.

Will everyone make a good impression on paper? No way! Everyone does not have the gift of writing or presentation. Does that mean they are not qualified? Absolutely not! Many qualified people are just not able to organize their achievement in an effective way. This is where you get the competitive edge by submitting a strong marketing tool and not an autobiography or simple job history to your prospective employer.

Human resources personnel and managers will take less than a minute to screen your resum鮠. Screening is the process they use to eliminate the people who they think do not match the job requirements. The first step is to separate the resum頳 before them into two piles: Selected and Rejected. Resum頳creening is conducted by matching the job applicant's skills, knowledge, and abilities with the job requirements. The "Accepted" pile is further divided into strong candidates and candidates with potential. The strong candidates will be called for an interview. The potential candidates may be called if nobody in the first group makes a favorable impression. Which category do you want to fall in?

Fact: Employers will want to see you on paper before requesting to meet you in person. If you do not look impressive on paper, you will not be contacted for an interview.

THE INTERVIEW

The next step in the recruitment process is to call the selected candidates for interviews. The interview process constitutes the tool most heavily used to determine who gets the job. That is why it should involve careful preparation. What should you do to gain the competitive edge in an interview?

Your Appearance

Dress for success. Remember image counts and people do judge you by the way you look. If you dress professionally, you will be more confident. Greater confidence coupled with adequate preparation will improve the way you respond to your interviewer.

Punctuality

Do not be late. If you do not know where the company is, take a test run prior to going on the interview. Do not arrive breathless. Give yourself time to fill out necessary paperwork prior to meeting with the interviewers.

Bring all your past employment information in an organized format to complete applications expeditiously.

Preparation

Research the company you will be interviewing with. Most interviewers will ask you what you know about the company or industry.

Get as much information as possible about the position you are applying for. You may be asked to explain why you are interested in doing the job.

Be prepared to give examples and explain accomplishments stated on your resum鮠. The person on the resum頡 and the one sitting before the interviewer should be the same people. Too often, people make the mistake of inflating their qualifications and cannot present themselves in the same light to the interviewer. Do not falsify information. The interviewer can usually tell if you are exaggerating. Remember honesty is still the best policy. Convey weaknesses in a positive manner.

Exhibit confidence instead of arrogance. There is a fine line between the two. Be genuine and leave off the airs.

Listen to the question that is asked of you. Do not be afraid to ask the interviewer to clarify a question you have difficulty understanding.

Convey to the interviewer what makes you unique. Know the strengths and assets that set you apart from the other candidates.

Remember every thing you say in the interview answers one general question, "Why should we hire you?"

Make sure you have questions for the interviewer. This shows your interest in the position as well as the company. Certainly there are things you want to know. Do not miss this opportunity to show your enthusiasm for the position.

Do not discuss salary in the interview. The appropriate time for discussing salary is after the hiring manager expresses that you are the selected one for the job.

Fact: While the resum頭 may get your feet in the door, acing the interview gives you the key to the job at a company.

Following Up

Do not forget your manners. Get business cards from the people you interview with. Send each one an individual thank you letter. While this does not guarantee you a job, a thank you or follow up letter provides an additional opportunity to sell your most valuable points prior to the hiring decision being made. It is also a chance for you to reconnect with the interviewer by reiterating some of the points that sold well during the interview.

Fact: Writing a follow up letter jogs the memory of the interviewer and may warrant them wanting to take a second look at you.

Job seekers should realize that merely developing and submitting a resum頤 does not guarantee them a job. However, putting the entire package of job search techniques together will help them to take the job search process to higher heights and beyond just a resum鮁.

Master Resume-writer and Resume Strategist Claudia A. Samuels Newton is the President and CEO of Rewarding Resume Services (http://www.rewardingresumes.com). Claudia has a Masters of Management in Human Resource Management degree and a Bachelors of Science degree in Business Administration. With over 20 years of industry experience, she has served hundreds of satisfied clients. Her speaking engagements include being a featured guest on WLTX TV in Columbia, SC and serving as a resume-writing consultant for higher education institutions in her community. Samuels-Newton provides online instruction in Communications as an Adjunct Faculty member for the University of Phoenix Online. She also serves in a management role at Blue-Choice HealthPlan, a subsidiary of BlueCross BlueShield of SC.

How to Make a Resume Stand Out

When applying for a job you need to keep in mind that a great resume by itself cannot land you a job. A bad and poorly done resume, on the other hand, can eliminate all your chances right away. If you want to learn how to make a resume stand out, here are some important tips to keep in mind.

- Your resume must be readable. You have to make sure that it is free of spelling and grammar mistakes, clean and precise. Hiring a professional to write the resume for you is a great solution but it's not always easy or doable. In any case, even if you are writing it yourself, keep in mind that the CV could be your only chance to impress someone; therefore, if it is sloppy or filled with mistakes that is what the prospective employer will think of you. A disorganized and careless employee is not attractive.

- Make sure that you are concise and precise about the positions you held at the previous companies. Do not avoid mentioning some jobs that are not necessarily similar to the one you are applying for; having a pertinent experience is always needed, but in some cases a person with different skills might be desired as well. Many companies look for a deep pool of employees and talents.

- Avoid common mistakes. Do not include your race or ethnicity in the resume. It is not legal for companies and employers to ask such things and base their decision on them. You should also avoid adding references. If the employer asks you to provide them you should be able to.

A resume is a marketing tool so it has to radiate excellence and precision. Details must stand out. Keep the basic format of a resume and try to point out your particular skills and talents.

Get more help on how to make a resume <http://www.squidoo.com/how-to_make_a_resume> and find lots of resume writing tips <http://www.squidoo.com/how-to_make_a_resume> .

A New Kind of Cover Letter For Your Job Search?

A Cover Letter 'Wizard' Always Asks the Magic Question!

You may not believe this but it's true. Thousands, maybe millions, of job-seekers spend hours preparing a cover letter to die for. And then it dies! Why? Because they neglect the one action step that makes all the difference. They don't ASK for an interview.

And those who remember to ask lack the 'magic' that results in a 'yes' from the hiring manager. "May I please come in for an interview-if you have time?" OR "Would you have time to meet with me?" OR "Would it be possible to have a moment of your time?"

Double 'duh' on all three. No magic. No spark. No confidence. No response.

But don't give up. I'm going to show you how to become a cover letter wizard by waving a wand of magic words that will bring you the golden interview you've been waiting for.

FOUR Magical Ways To ASK For The Job Interview

1. Write a great HEADLINE in bold and center it directly above your greeting.

May we get together to discuss the position of [fill in job opening title here]?

2. Focus on YOUR QUALIFICATIONS in the beginning of your letter.

The position of general manager is just what I'm looking for. I'd love the opportunity to meet with you in person to discuss your needs and requirements. Here are some of the responsibilities I've held over the past five years. As you can see, my background has prepared me well for this type of position.

3. Be SPECIFIC ABOUT TIME in your final paragraph.

If possible, I'd like to schedule an interview with you in the next two weeks. I'm available Tuesday, Wednesday and Thursday afternoons between 1:00 and 5:00 p.m. Do any of these work for you? I promise to keep our meeting short and specific. I will arrive prepared to show you what I can accomplish within the first month and how I can meet your needs for the position of general manager.

4. Communicate YOUR ENTHUSIASM at the end of your letter.

I am excited to meet with you. [Company name] is the company I'd really like to work for. To schedule an interview you can reach me on my cell phone at: 555-555-5555. I really look forward to meeting with you.

Give up waiting and hoping. Wave that magic wand over your next cover letter and show the hiring manager you mean business! Remember to ASK for the job interview clearly, directly and sincerely every single time.

2009 Copyright, Written By Jimmy Sweeney; President of CareerJimmy and Author of the Amazing Cover Letter Creator

Jimmy Sweeney is the president of CareerJimmy and author of several career related books and writes a monthly article titled, "Job Search Secrets"

Want even more free cover letter tips <http://www.coverlettercentral.com/jimmy-sweeney-cover-letters.htm> from Jimmy Sweeney? Get *loads* of free advice to help write great cover letters ... visit http://www.coverlettercentral.com/jimmy-sweeney-cover-letters.htm now

Do You Make This Cover Letter Mistake?

Everyone enjoys a word of endearment. Dear Hiring Manager can be a warm and friendly way to start a cover letter to a prospective employer. However, there is nothing as near and dear to one's ear-and heart--as the sound of one's name. So from now on use the personal touch when you greet the person you're writing to. This is the fastest way to bring your cover letter to the top of the mail pile.

Which of the following greetings is most effective?

Example #1:

Dear Ms. Allen
Dear John Smith
Dear Mrs. Preston

Example #2:

Dear Hiring Manager
Dear HR Director
Dear Personnel Supervisor

Example #3:

To whom it may concern:

Clearly, the best of the three examples is the one with the individuals' names. But if you don't have a specific name, then address the man or woman by a company title. Example #3 is of no concern because it doesn't concern anyone in particular! Never use this greeting. It lacks care, warmth, and professionalism. Take time to find out the name of the employer you wish to reach (call the company or check the web site for that information) and then use this little-known secret-greeting him or her by a first name.

One More Secret-To Use In Case Of Emergency!
If you cannot get a specific name, use one of the greetings in Example #2 and add this personal note.

PLEASE NOTE: I apologize for not addressing you by name. I was unable to get this information online or by phone. I'm very interested in the position of [insert job title here] and I look forward to the opportunity to meet with you in person for an interview.

Such a message would surely motivate him or her to call you for an interview. This 'secret' alone turns a negative into a positive that will work for you. So before you write your next cover letter, ask yourself this important question: Who will want to hear what I have to say? Then find out that name and write a great cover letter starting with 'Dear.'

2009 Copyright, Written By Jimmy Sweeney; President of CareerJimmy and Author of the Amazing Cover Letter Creator

Jimmy Sweeney is the president of CareerJimmy and author of several career related books and writes a monthly article titled, "Job Search Secrets"

Want even more free cover letter tips <http://www.coverlettercentral.com/jimmy-sweeney-cover-letters.htm> from Jimmy Sweeney? Get *loads* of free advice to help write great cover letters... visit http://www.coverlettercentral.com/jimmy-sweeney-cover-letters.htm now.

A Cover Letter That Hits the Bull's-Eye!

If a one-page cover letter is good, a two-page letter is even better? Absolutely not. Employers are busy professionals who have just a moment or two to look over your cover letter-so it's important to make your point-on one page.

How To Say A LOT in a LITTLE Space

It's not as difficult as it seems. Less really is more-when it comes to crafting a cover letter that's a direct hit. It's a simple matter of focusing your time and attention on the essentials-the items an employer is most interested in. Here's how you can do just that.

Use these SEVEN magical KEYS to unlock a successful Cover Letter

1. Create three paragraphs on one page. First, state the job you want. Second, list your qualifications. And third, clearly and directly ASK for the opportunity to be interviewed for the job.
2. Limit each paragraph to three or four well-written sentences.
3. Leave generous margins so there's plenty of white space and be sure to double space between paragraphs.
4. Help the reader see at a glance what you wish to say by using numbers or bullets.
5. Bold-face the first sentence of each paragraph to capture attention.
6. Read through to catch errors, then print it out for one final edit.
7. Remember, a one-page carefully-crafted cover letter has the best chance of hitting the "Bull's-Eye!"

Imagine how the employer will feel when he opens your cover letter--a simple, clearly worded letter that contains only necessary information and directly asks for the job interview as well.

Unlock The Golden Door

There you have it. SEVEN KEYS to a successful cover letter that will motivate any employer to read yours from beginning to end, then reach for the phone and call you for an interview that could very well lead to being hired for the job you've been dreaming of.

Pick up these keys today and unlock your future with an amazing cover letter!

2009 Copyright, Written By Jimmy Sweeney; President of CareerJimmy and Author of the Amazing Cover Letter Creator

Jimmy Sweeney is the president of CareerJimmy and author of several career related books and writes a monthly article titled, "Job Search Secrets"

Want even more free cover letter tips <http://www.coverlettercentral.com/jimmy-sweeney-cover-letters.htm> from Jimmy Sweeney? Get *loads* of free advice to help write great cover letters ... visit http://www.coverlettercentral.com/jimmy-sweeney-cover-letters.htm now.

Cover Letter Sample

When you are applying for a cover letter, you should be sure of what to write. You should also review the letter after composing it. This is basically the first impression you can make to your potential employers. Your cover letter must indicate which position you're applying for, your skills and your experiences.

Here is a sample of a cover letter.

James Macintosh
Rain Company
47829 Maine Street
Los Angeles, CA 90210

Dear Mr. Macintosh

I have always wanted to teach and I have accomplished this as soon as I finish my college education. In order for me to add more to my knowledge and abilities, I continued educating myself by volunteering in various schools. There, I practice what I've learned.

I can work on my own or be a part of a team. I have enough motivation to provide your company the best service. I can deliver on time. I am fluent in Spanish.

Other skills I can offer are:

1. My knowledge on health disorders

2. My teaching and counseling principles

3. My ability to mediate between clients and agencies

I have also done surveys and mapping tasks which concentrates on foundation formation and soul mechanics. I have dabbled in analysis and structural design of the school in our town.

I was encouraged by Cynthia Rowley, Director of California University, to send in my application to the position of English Teacher. After careful study of your school, I am confident that I can provide you my services in the best way possible.

You can contact me at the phone number and email address I have indicated below. I look forward to hearing from you. I can be reached anywhere and anytime. Thank you for your consideration.

As seen here, an effective cover letter explains the reasons why you are interested in the organization. It must also indicate the position you are applying for. In connection to this, the skills that have been enumerated must go well with the position being applied for because the company hires possible employees on what they can offer.

The cover letter is reviewed by the employer. The intention is to identify why the applicant is applying for and seeking out the position with the company. The cover letter is the critical phase on the job search procedure. This is the opportunity to get the attention and the interest of the employer.

Tips to writing an effective cover letter:

1. Your opening paragraph must be attention grabbing since this is the first part the potential reader would notice.

2. Use bullet points in indicating your skills.In this way, you wouldn't have to use "I" too much. The employer would also have an easier time reading these.

3. Mention accomplishments that show how qualified you are to the position you're applying for.

4. Head straight to the point and do not dilly dally. The employer has no time for nonsense. The more direct your cover letter is, the better chance of you getting that interview.

5. Name dropping is effective. The person you mention need not be working in the company. He or she can be someone the reader respects.

6. Be proactive when requesting for interviews. If you are going to follow up, then follow up. If the employer arranged a time for you to call, call at that time.

2009 Copyright, Written By Jimmy Sweeney; President of CareerJimmy and Author of the Amazing Cover Letter Creator

Jimmy Sweeney is the president of CareerJimmy and author of several career related books and writes a monthly article titled, "Job Search Secrets"

Want even more free cover letter tips <http://www.coverlettercentral.com/jimmy-sweeney-cover-letters.htm> from Jimmy Sweeney? Get *loads* of free advice to help write great cover letters ... visit http://www.coverlettercentral.com/jimmy-sweeney-cover-letters.htm now

Discussing an Example of a Cover Letter - And the Importance of It

Cover letters serves as introduction statements to such occasions like baptism, birthdays, weddings, funerals and other social gatherings. Usually cover letters accompany invitation cards and it is placed before it; it is like a "read-me-first" note that gives either excitement or depth on a situation, depending on the appropriate commotion. Example of a cover letter might be an enclosed love letter to a wedding invitation, a bible verse for a christening, a happy quotation for a birthday party invitation card, or even a eulogy for a sad funeral occasion. If that isn't the purpose of cover letters, well, I'm not what could be its purpose then.

Society never runs out of these kinds of things that make a civilized world civilize, we need these cover letters to give importance to the things that are important to us, and make us who we are. What are we anyways? Well I'm human and I'm sure the one who reads this next is a human being same as me. If there's a girl thing, and a boy thing, there surely is a "human thing". The use of cover letters is positively one of these examples that I want to point out. Anyways, the term "human thing" that I had just used is quite easy to figure out, and I'm sure you already did that, but to put this thought to word "human thing" is a simplified term that I would want to use to explain the complexities of human norms, that without it, we can never be human at all.

In a quest to know what is a human letter, the first thing we should do is have a example of a cover letter, why is it appropriate to a certain occasion, why is it not to other occasion and why is it used. Moreover, an example that surely everyone will be pleased to discuss is a cover love letter, why is it important? Is it important in the first place? I'm sure it is, if you are a guy, and you plan to ask a girl's hand in marriage, how beautiful can it be to have a love letter in your hand? Picture this; you have this love letter, you gave it to your girlfriend, and when she finished reading it, she could be laughing, for she's feeling a bit of bliss, then you showed her a ring and popped the question! Only a foolish girl will deny you of the moment, or maybe she doesn't love you... that is a different story that I'm glad to share with you on another good time. The point in here is how a cover letter indicates an important moment, just like the one we had in our example of a cover letter.

Mark Mattey is a writer and entrepreneur. To learn more about cover letter examples <http://www.coverlettersthatkill.com> or examples of cover letters <http://www.coverlettersthatkill.com> , visit his website.

How to Make a Cover Letter - Insider Secrets of Making an Effective Cover Letter

There are around hundreds of resumes that come in everyday when there is any opening in the company and sometimes the companies also consider revising the other left out resumes which were not attended before. In this type of scenario, where the HR people do not spend much time on reading what's inside your resume, your cover letter has to be really impressive and an only on in hundreds which catches the eyes of the reader.

Cover letter is basically a small description about the person who is applying for a job. Generally HR managers do not have time to pick up and read every resume and then call for the interview. Only people who get qualified for the interview are the ones, who have submitted a very acceptable cover letter along with the resume.

Here are some insider secrets of making an effective cover letter:

1. The first and the most important tip to note is that your cover letter should always be short and precise. For keeping it short, you do not need to eradicate the useful information, but mention your point sin a smart way. Fro e.g.: when telling about your post in the organization and your working style etc; do not write a whole paragraph. Instead always explain the same in not more than 2 lines.

2. Second important thing to keep in mind is that your cover letter should not be the basic one as sent by all other people. You have to make it unique. Mention the key points of the company for which you are giving the interview. Try telling the interviewee in your cover letter that how you are the most appropriate of all candidates for this job.

3. Keep your cover letter in bullets and points. Keeping bullets and points makes it easy for the person to read. Bold the subheads if any, so that the moment HR manager opens your letter his/her eyes are directly attracted towards the information mentioned in the points.

4. Now is the time to end the letter. The last paragraph of the letter must specify that they must read your CV as there is a lot more that needs to be figured out.

Just Applying for jobs may not be enough, you also need try online businesses to add new income sources. Try the free trial for Google Cash & learn the secret for earning thousands of dollars per month online.

Go here --> Google Cash Free Trial <http://www.loanratemodifications.com>

President Obama has come up with Stimulus Package that will focus on providing assistance to low- and middle-income Americans, to check if you qualify for Government Grants

Go here --> Federal Grant Programs <http://www.loanratemodifications.com>

FREE Trials are for a limited time only, so get yours today

Creating a Cover Letter - Steps to Create a Professional Resume Cover Letter

If you want to make the first impression on your employer, create an effective cover letter. A cover letter always increases your chance to get noticed. Nowadays employers are flooded with thousands of resumes for one particular post. There is a huge competition in the market but with an expressive and focused cover letter, half of the battle is already won.

Cover letters can give your employer a nice glimpse of yours. Employers always appreciate a nicely written cover letter. After working in your resume, you can write it, which will compliment your resume. So let's create a cover letter which will not only give us a job but also lots of appreciation.

Steps to create a professional resume cover letter

It is always advisable to use simpler and shorter sentences. Each paragraph should not exceed more than three to four sentences.

You should always take care of the proper format. It starts with your contact information at top left side of the page, followed by date, employer contact Information (if any), salutation, body , first, second and third paragraph, complimentary close and your signature.

The body of the job application letter allows employer to know the position you have applied as per your key strengths. The first paragraph should tell about your interest towards the organization. You can also include the name of a mutual contact , if any.

The second paragraph is all about connecting a link between you and your employer. It should be persuasive and should appeal to the employer's need. The final paragraph should be a kind of thank you note. You can thank your employers for investing their precious time with your job application form

Proof read it after a gap and then send it along with your resume.

In Today's Job Market - First Impressions Are Very Important

In today's job market, first impressions are very important. That's why your resume and cover letter should be top notch and perfect. When you present yourself to a prospective new employer, you want them to think highly of you by first looking at your resume and cover letter.

Let's start with your resume. You want your resume to stand out above all the rest. Think about it from the prospective employer's point of view for just a minute. He now has an open position for whatever reason, which is unknown to us. He puts an ad in the local paper or online job board and starts to receive resumes to consider for the first round of interviews. With the amount of people out of a job at the moment, he may have 400 to 500 resumes to go through. Boy that is a lot of reading! How does he begin to weed out the bad ones and keep the great ones? One of the things he looks for is a lot of bang for his bucks. In other words, he wants a full packed resume that takes up as little paper as possible. No matter how well a resume looks, if it has more than two pages, it probably will get thrown out. The prospective employer will get bored and lose interest very quickly, as he knows he has a lot of resumes to go through.

If you write your resume correctly and compactly, you can get everything you need to convey in one to two pages at most. One thing that will help is to only list your past employers and the position you held. If the prospective employer wants to know more about what you did, he will ask at the time of your interview. Don't list out your references; just let it be known that they are available.

Now, for your cover letter, again be short, sweet and to the point. Introduce yourself briefly; advise of the job you are applying for and tell them, you look forward to hearing from them soon. Don't use fancy paper, as they don't really impress anyone but you. And in these days and times, you will probably be faxing your resume to the number listed in the advertisement.

Think positive and be prepared to be called in for an interview!

Mark Rozados
Info@findajobinyourstate.com
</Info@findajobinyourstate.com>

What is a Perfect Cover Letter?

If you want to learn about writing the "perfect" cover letter, then this article was written for you.

The definition of a cover letter includes words like introduction, presentation and motivation. A cover letter must has all these characteristics.

The goal of the letter is to introduce yourself and present the particular attributes and work experience you possess that make you particularly qualified for a position. It is a perfect cover letter if the the reader is motivated to review your resume more closely than the other 500 they received , and contact you specifically for an interview.

Numerous websites populate the internet with detailed instructions on how to write cover letters. There are a plethora of samples that cover every job position and employment situation experienced by mankind.

The raw material is there but it's up to you to shape the stock forms into a motivating presentation. At a minimum the perfect cover letter contains the name of the president or human resource director for the company you are applying to, some information revealing your knowledge of their company, the specific reason you are a qualified prospect for the position and conveys a high interest in winning the position. This needs to be done in one or two paragraphs on one sheet of paper.

Write with the interests of the company in mind. Promote how you can improve the bottom line, further their cause, or strengthen their position. Take the time it requires to develop these key elements and you will be on your way to writing the perfect cover letter every time.

If you're looking for quality cover letters <http://www.coverletters.genuinefeedback.org> , you should take a look at my blog - where I'll show you the best resource available for creating an awesome cover letter in just a few minutes - Your phone will be ringing off the hook with job offers if you use these templates, guaranteed. Go here <http://www.coverletters.genuinefeedback.org> to go there now.

Sample Cover Letters For Resumes - Tips For What to Look For

If you're looking for sample cover letters for resume, then this article is going to show you exactly where to find them.

It's like socks and shoes: One without the other says something about the person. A resume without a cover letter indicates the person doesn't know business protocol or chooses not to comply with it. Either way prospective employers are not interested. There are droves of sample cover letters for resumes on the internet today. Taking the time to find one that fits your style and making it yours with some tactful changes and addition of your information is easy enough to do.

There are several general types of cover letters. If you have the specific job and company information to which you are submitting a resume, you want to look at targeted cover letters. A prospecting letter is the one used when you are sending your resume to a company and asking if they could use your experience or skills. A third type of cover letter used for resumes is the networking cover letter. This type of letter is a request for help and insight in your job search efforts.

You can easily find sample cover letters at almost every college, job search and career development site on the internet. They are often broken down into subcategories of job titles or situations - which is perfect for finding the right one.

The samples can introduce you to power phases related to the employment field you are addressing. Others help with wording for situations that could be considered difficult such as changing careers, being a new college graduate, or re-entering the work force.

If you're looking for quality cover letters <http://www.coverletters.genuinefeedback.org> , you should take a look at my blog - where I'll show you the best resource available for creating an awesome cover letter in just a few minutes - Your phone will be ringing off the hook with job offers if you use these templates, guaranteed. Go here <http://www.coverletters.genuinefeedback.org> to go there now.

Submitting Your Resume is Not Enough - Make Sure Your Resume Gets Read

As unemployment continues to soar and more and more people are out 'looking for a job,' I feel compelled to share some insight into the job search process - particularly as it relates to resumes and job boards. Now I realize that there are many different theories on resume writing and cover letters however, with 15 years experience in the recruiting and employment market, I think can offer some insight.

Almost every job seeker I have spoken to has submitted resumes to multiple job postings online. It makes me cringe when I hear that. Yes, but if I don't apply how will I ever get a chance at the interview? I understand the logic, however, job seekers need to know a few things about the resume submittal process.

Almost all sizable companies have an applicant tracking system (ATS). What does this mean for you?

1. Your resume and cover letter may or may not make it to the same file in the company's ATS.
2. Your resume if not 'formatted correctly' for the company's system may only be viewed as a text document with no formatting - one flow of words - almost unreadable.
3. Most recruiters will search for your submitted resume through key words. If you resume does not have the key words they are looking for, you won't be found.

How can you remedy this?

1. If you are submitting a resume to an ad online, skip the cover letter. Chances are, it won't be read. Companies are inundated with 100's of resumes for most job postings. Making sure your resume makes it in front of a live person is challenging enough.

2. Make sure your resume is formatted in Microsoft Word. Skip the PDF format. Most ATS systems cannot convert those files. Your resume will get lost in translation.
3. Make sure you have specific key words from the job posting sprinkled in your resume. You want to be found, don't you?

4. Find the name of either the hiring manager or recruiter who is handling this position. Make sure that you call and leave a voice mail with your name, phone number and elevator pitch (including the title of the job applied for) 2-3 days after submitting your resume. Most hiring managers/recruiters will look up your name in the database and take a look at your resume if your message is compelling enough. If you don't hear back (and unless you are a perfect fit for the role on paper, you won't) call back one week later and leave one additional message. No more. Desperation calling is creepy.

Better yet, skip the resume submission process and find a way to get introduced to the hiring manager through a networking contact, industry event or Linkedin.

While resumes are the popular way to feel as if you are actively conducting a job search, unless you take specific steps to follow up, you are wasting your time.

Ginni Garner is the Owner and Managing Director of Sanford Rose Associates - Cleveland East. Sanford Rose Associates, has served the recruitment needs of clients for senior-level executives and professionals for over fifty years. □?The Cleveland East provides executive and management recruitment services as well as outplacement services for companies in Ohio and across the globe. Visit http://www.srexecutivesearch.com

Resume Writing - What's In And What's Out

If you haven't written a resume in awhile, you may not be current on the trends in resume writing. You need to know what's in and what's out so that you don't make costly mistakes when writing your resume.

What's in

Professional summaries are in and have been for several years now. A professional summary highlights a job seeker's best assets and positions that person for the type of job that he or she is seeking. It has also become common to list core competencies (or keywords) underneath the summary so that the resume is more likely to be found by a recruiter or hiring manager after it has been scanned into a database.

Accomplishments are definitely in. A resume without crisply worded, powerful accomplishment statements is not likely to be noticed. Many job seekers make the mistake of simply listing their duties. But a laundry list of duties makes a job seeker sound like everyone else who has done similar work. Accomplishments distinguish you from your competition. And they show that you have actually made a contribution to the organization's bottom line.

ASCII versions of your resume are in. Since job seekers often have to submit their information through an online form, it is best to have an ASCII version of your resume in addition to a Word version. The formatting in a Word document gets distorted when copied and pasted onto an online form, which is why the ASCII version is useful. The ASCII version is just plain text without the formatting. With ASCII you don't have to worry about a bullet showing up on the other end as some other type of symbol.

What's out

A job objective is out for people who have experience in the field that they are applying for jobs in. If your work history supports your job objective, it's not necessary to state that job objective explicitly on the resume.

References available upon request is out. It used to be standard as the last line on the resume, but now it is obsolete. It is simply expected that you will supply your references at the time of the interview.

Hobbies are out if they are unrelated to your job objective. You may really be a skydiving enthusiast, but if you are applying for a job as an accountant, it's probably not worth mentioning in this setting.

Personal information is out. I still see resumes where people put their marital status and number of children. This is information that employers cannot ask about, and it is not information that should be included in a resume.

Leaving large gaps of time unexplained on the resume is unacceptable. If the gap is longer than three months, you need to account for the time somehow. If you did volunteer work during this time or stayed home with children, you can write this up so that you show job related skills.

Cheryl Palmer, M.Ed. is a certified career coach and a professional resume writer. She has been a guest on a radio show entitled How to Find a Job Fast hosted by Chris Russell where she discussed tips for finding employment more quickly in this economic downturn. In addition, she was a guest on the radio show "Balance and Wisdom" where she discussed networking for your career with hosts Barbara Phillips and Joanie Winberg.

In an article on HotJobs' website entitled "The Art of Being Assertive," Cheryl was quoted as a subject matter expert on how assertiveness can help a person advance in his or her career. She was also quoted in an article on CNN: "What Says to an Employer, 'Hire Me!'"

Resumes - US Vs French

Mirror, mirror on the wall who is the fairest of them all? The issue of someone's physical appearance affecting whether or not they get a job offer is not new. In fact, there have been many cases in which this has been a central issue. I was given an assignment in one of my classes, which involved me reading about a woman who was preparing to apply for a job. She spoke about putting her resum頴 together. She needed to decide what to say about her previous jobs, which picture of herself to include, etc. This shocked me. She was not only required to include a photograph of herself in her resum鬠, but she also had to state whether she was single or married. This is simply unheard of in the U.S. However, in France it is considered normal.

I brought this matter up in class the next day because I was curious about whether she was looking for a job or a date for Friday night. My professor said that although requiring that type of information to be included would be considered to be a form of discrimination in the U.S, it is not viewed that way in France. I found the prospect of being required to submit such information offensive, and I was feeling quite pleased to live in a country that does not require that type of information to be included in a resum鮠. A moment later, I was faced with a rather harsh reality check. My professor said that we do the same things here in the U.S.; we are just more subtle about it. If you just look at someone's resum鬠, you can discover pretty much the same things that a photo will tell you. For instance, often times a person's name will reveal what their nationality is. If you look at the date of their graduation, you can guess their age pretty accurately. The rest will all be revealed at the job interview.

The French like to know about the whole package before they hire a person. That is why their resum鱯s typically include how many children they have, their marital status, etc. This gives the potential employer a better idea of where the person is in his/her life. There is more to life than merely working for a living and, whether we would like to admit it or not, personal lives do affect work lives. For instance, someone who is single may have more freedom to switch jobs due to having fewer personal obligations than a married person. This may lead to a higher turnover rate than if the company hired more married people. A more typical concern for women is that companies will discriminate against them if they feel that the women are likely to become pregnant. This concerns American's because they see that type of information as something that could cause discrimination during the hiring process.

American's try to keep their work lives separate from their private lives. Their resum鱯s contain their various accomplishments such as awards received, jobs held, degrees awarded, etc. They are not typically personal in nature. The goal is to show what you have done, not who you are. After a potential employer decides that the accomplishments are suitably impressive, the individual is invited on an interview. This is where the individual will display his/her personal traits. Although, the interview usually focuses on what the person is like to work with, not what they do in their spare time. This makes the potential employee feel like he/she is being evaluated solely on his/her professional abilities.

The issue of discrimination during the hiring process is an important one; however, it is important to note that very few companies will hire someone without having met with them at least once. Most, if not all, of these personal questions will be answered by the end of that meeting, even if there are no specific questions asked regarding them. Discrimination in the work place and during the hiring process will always be an issue, but it is not necessarily a very personal resum頴 that will keep an individual from obtaining a job. It may keep them from obtaining an interview though.

Christie Pate is a student at West Chester University completing her Accounting degree.

Effective Cover Letters - Secrets to Writing Great Cover Letters and Landing That Job!

If you want to learn the secrets of effective cover letters, then this article was written for you. Specifically, we're going to look at how to make your letter stand out, how important this part of your application really is, and why you should consider using a template.

Let's start by talking about how important it is for you to stand out. Chances are, your potential employers are going to see a lot of cover letters, and most of them will just be glanced over without a second thought. So you need to make yours attention grabbing. Make sure they can't just forget you!

This doesn't mean you should lie, though. There's really no need either - lying is counter productive. Instead, put yourself in their shoes - what would grab your attention in a good way?

Next, you need to realize how important the your letter really is. You see, most people think it's just a formality. But they couldn't be further from the truth if they tried. Your letter is the first impression you make - it sets the scene for reading your resume. The hiring manager is busy, and is probably not having fun reading through dozens of boring, generic cover letters. Make sure your one isn't a chore to read.

Finally, let's talk about using templates. You see, there's really no need to reinvent the wheel. It's fine to use a template. Don't make it obvious, though - by using a boring generic template with no additional thought or effort put into it. If you're a good writer, then you should write your own letter. But if you're not, take the initiative and find a good cover letter template to work from.

In this day and age it's hard enough to get a new job. Don't make it harder for yourself by not putting some effort into this crucial aspect of your application.

If you're looking for effective cover letters <http://www.coverletters.genuinefeedback.org> , you should take a look at my blog - where I'll show you the best resource available for creating an awesome cover letter in just a few minutes - Your phone will be ringing off the hook with job offers if you use these templates, guaranteed. Go here <http://www.coverletters.genuinefeedback.org> to go there now.

Online Printing Your Resume

We have heard all about the terrible effects of the recession to the livelihood of many. Companies all over the world are downsizing. As such, the result is that we have heard a lot of stories about someone losing a job and the difficulty of finding one. In situations like this, one has to be prepared always.

If you have just lost your job and you are now searching for another job opportunity, and then continue reading this because it might help you land a good one.

Resumes are important in job hunting because it is the first contact with your potential employer. It is therefore commonsensical to put your best foot forward. Mass produced resumes do not work. You have to clearly understand this. It has to be tailored according to the descriptions of the particular job or employment you are applying for. It is therefore necessary to customize every resume or cover letter to the requirements of the company.

Always remember that your resume and cover letter are your primary supporting documents that will be able to convince employers that you are the one they are looking for. Nevertheless, despite of you being the best candidate, you would not be able to get the job unless your resume, cover letter and interview skills stand out. These would help you a great deal in selling yourself and negotiating with the best offer.

There are online printing websites that can help you build a professional and solid resume. The good thing here is you have the option to choose from among the many options online and customize it according to your requirements. You just have to input personal information in the pre-formatted layout and then you choose how you like the interplay of fonts and colors.

Some of the best online printing websites offer to take care of all aspects of resume writing. There are often unlimited versions of a resume outline provided, as well as ready-made cover letter formats that can be further edited and tailored down to tie in your best qualifications to the particular description of the employment you are applying for. There are even those that notify and remind you through emails of the things you need to do after sending your resume. One online printing website even reminds clients to make follow up calls!

You can preview your resume before printing online. Proof reading your resume can be easily performed at any point. Upon editing, you can print it online or save it for printing later. The trick here is to constantly update your resume so that you will not forget to put in any important additions that may help your resume improve a lot better.

In just a few minutes and with a mouse visit, you are on your way to creating that resume that will land you a job. Online printing can help you impress even the most discriminating employer and put you ahead of the competition. Printing online can definitely help you get a head start on that dream position.

Kaye Z. Marks is an avid writer and follower of the developments in online printing <http://www.printplace.com> and printing online <http://www.printplace.com> industry.

Creating Resumes For Temporary Positions

Whether landing a job that is permanent or temporary, you must have a resume that fits the position so that you can land the job. If you are one of those individuals who seeks out just temporary positions, then using the same resume for each job is not going to suffice. Some very important points can be missed in that resume, so it is important that you know how to write resumes for temporary positions.

Here is how you are going to construct your resume:

Use a high quality paper. Office supply stores and department stores carry resume paper, which is of a higher stock and very professional.

Make sure you understand the job description. You need to point out the areas in the job description that you are qualified to do. So study it well so that you can apply what you read to your resume.

Go ahead and lay out your resume, starting with your objectives, your past job experience, your educational background, skills, volunteer experience, any licenses or publications, and references.

Now you're going to fill in the gaps. Your objective is what you hope to accomplish by acquiring the position. Your skills are about any skills that you have acquired, such as computer skills and customer service skills. If you have ever volunteered for anything, make sure you include that because it shows how diverse you are. Adding references is also a great way to add to your credibility.

When it comes to the work experience section, this is where you need to be careful. This is where you are to take what you evaluated in the job description and highlight what you have done in past jobs that apply to the job description. You want to emphasize that you are able to do the job that you are wishing to acquire.

In the education section, you want to record your education. If you were in clubs or involved in certain activities, make sure you list those things to add to your qualifications. You'll be surprised how much this can help.

When you package up the resume, make sure you don't staple it or paper clip it together. It is very important that the resume remain in perfect condition. If you must mail the resume, make sure you put it in a manila envelope and remove the closure prongs because the postal service will make you remove them anyway.

The goal of creating such a resume is to show the employer that you are the best candidate for the job. Imagine submitting the same resume to every possible employer and how you could be missing some very valuable points on your resume. Unfortunately, this is a mistake that nearly everyone makes. They simply put everything they possibly can on the resume in hopes that something will stand out to the potential employer.

It is important to realize that employers scan resumes before they fully read them. They are looking for something that stands out to them and it's not so much fancy fonts and pretty borders. They are looking at the text of the resume to see if there is a skill or qualification that you have that will really get the job done for them.

Although this seems like a lot of work, make sure you put in that time. That is how you are going to be able to land your temporary jobs almost every single time. In the end, the time you put in is worth it. You'll be doing a great temporary job in no time and you'll have a lot of fun doing it.

Temp Agency <http://www.drakeintl.com/ca/> offering staff solutions and Human Resources Consulting <http://www.drakeintl.com/ca/bussolutions/hraudit.aspx> company that will help to reach your business' objective.

Best Cover Letter Format

For you to be able to make an effective cover letter, you should be able to follow at least the basic format which should never fail to address three general issues:

1. First Paragraph - The reason why you are writing
2. Middle Paragraphs - Facts about what you have to offer
3. Concluding Paragraph - Methods for you to follow-up

In the first cover letter format, you should give the real reason why you are writing to the company. You have to express your enthusiasm and you should be able to match your credentials with the position's qualifications so the employer will also become eager to hire you.

In the second part, express your credentials and abilities. Take note of all those things that you can offer. As much as possible, refer to the qualifications listed on their advertisement and try to illustrate how your abilities can relate to the position. In writing this part of the cover letter, it would help if you can put your best foot forward.

The concluding paragraph of every correct cover letter format is for you to again express your interest over the job and allow your employer to understand how they will be able to reach you. Give your phone number and/or email address. If you can, it would be nice if you can come to their office after a couple of weeks so you can inquire about the status of your job application.

Be professional in your cover letter; avoid unnecessary wordings and graphics on the paper. The simpler it is then the better.

Jimmy Sweeney is the President of CareerJimmy and author of the brand new, Amazing Cover Letter Creator <http://www.amazing-cover-letters.com/> Visit Jimmy on the web at: http://www.amazing-cover-letters.com for your "instant" cover.

Right Cover Letter Template

To obtain the best interest of your possible employer, you should follow the right cover letter template before you submit your resume. It is necessary that you follow the right trend in writing so you do not end up having something that looks awfully stupid for an employee.

In every cover letter template, you have to write the information on how an employer will be able to contact you on the first section. In case you have contact information for the employer then you can also include that. If not, you can simply list your information.

On the first paragraph, you should write about the real reason why you are writing. It is also necessary to mention the position that you wish to apply for. In the middle paragraph, you should tackle about some facts on what you have to offer for the employer. You should be able to convince your reader that you are the right person for the job. To conclude your cover letter, show your gratitude by thanking your employee for being able to consider you for such position. You should also put the necessary information on how you will follow-up in case the employer wishes to conduct a personal assessment on you. Indicate what you will do and write the time when you are going to do your follow-up.

For your concluding statement, you should write your name and your signature for formality. Following this cover letter template will give you an edge among any other applicants since most employers would like to have someone who is as professional as one could be.

Jimmy Sweeney is the President of CareerJimmy and author of the brand new, Amazing Cover Letter Creator <http://www.amazing-cover-letters.com/> Visit Jimmy on the web at: http://www.amazing-cover-letters.com for your "instant" cover.

Guide to Teacher Cover Letter

Applying for a teaching position is relatively an easy work if you know the right works to put on your teacher cover letter. For you to be able to land on the job that you want then you should be able to stand out in the midst of millions of applicants that are also looking at the job.

For you to get noticed by your employer, you can begin to list down your list of your achievements that you've garnered over the past few years. Furthermore, you can also include some of the seminars that you have attended. The problem with a lot of applicants is that they fail to give a cover letter together with a resume hence the employer would most likely choose those people who were able to give them this letter. Without any doubt, a teacher cover letter is a great addition to your resume if you want to get noticed.

But not all people are knowledgeable when it comes to writing hence it would help a lot if you can have something that will serve as your basis for writing. However, you don't need to copy everything that is written on the original cover letter since it will be very awkward. Beside who knows if your employer will run your script in a plagiarism checker? Be creative and be resourceful as much as possible. Continue writing your resume until the time comes when you are able to land on the perfect cover letter that you can use on your own.

Jimmy Sweeney is the President of CareerJimmy and author of the brand new, Amazing Cover Letter Creator <http://www.amazing-cover-letters.com/> Visit Jimmy on the web at: http://www.amazing-cover-letters.com for your "instant" cover.

Ways to Write a Cover Letter

It is entirely hard to write, particularly if you are going to write something with a formal note. If you try to analyze things, you will realize that one of the hardest methods of writing is doing a cover letter hence a lot of people are searching on how to write a cover letter over the internet so they could understand how to simplify the process.

As a rule of the thumb, a cover letter must be something that will complement and not duplicate your resume. This should be written with a purpose of interpreting the data-oriented, accurate resume in order to add up a personal touch.

There are 3 types of cover letter which includes:

? The application letter which tackle about a known job opening
? The prospecting letter which is created to inquire about a possible position
? The networking letter that is used to request information in your job search.

The right way on how to write a cover letter is to explain the main reason behind your interest about a certain position and you should understand your most relevant skill that would help you get the job. As much as possible, express high interest towards the position so your employer will realize that you will become a good asset to your company. You should also learn about the right way to format your letter so your employer will understand that you are professional enough for the job. You see, writing a cover letter is easy just as long as you try to organize your thoughts.

Jimmy Sweeney is the President of CareerJimmy and author of the brand new, Amazing Cover Letter Creator <http://www.amazing-cover-letters.com/> Visit Jimmy on the web at: http://www.amazing-cover-letters.com for your "instant" cover.

Ways to Write a Resume

How to write a resume - this is one big question that most applicants are faced with. As scary as the question may sound, this is actually easy if you just gear yourself with the right information that you need. First of all, you need to take note about your work experience. Include those unpaid works and part time since they can create a good impression on your resume. Next, take note about your education and job title that you have acquired through time.

Note some of your job accomplishments, specially those major ones. You can also list you membership on certain organizations, special accomplishments, and military service if there is any. From your list of skills, look for those that are transferable or those skills that are somehow relevant to the job opening that you are applying for.

Start your resume writing by putting on your full name, address, fax, telephone number, and email. Create a good objective that should be made in short sentences that describe the kind of work that you wish to obtain. After then, write down your work experience with your recent job. Don't forget to include the name of the company and the responsibilities that you hold in your job.

Always focus on your skills that you think is helpful for the new company that you are applying on. You can also include relevant information about you like computer programming knowledge, languages spoken, etc. under the heading. Then you can follow other vital information about yourself. You can look for resume examples over the internet so you will be guided well.

Jimmy Sweeney is president of CareerJimmy and author of the brand new, Amazing Resume Creator <http://www.amazingresumecreator.com/> In just 10 minutes flat you can quickly and easily CREATE or UPDATE your resume without spending a lot of money. Just a few visits of your mouse turns an "average" resume into an AMAZING resume guaranteed to land you more hot job interviews next week. Learn how to stand out from the crowd of job seekers <http://www.amazingresumecreator.com/> and attract the attention of Hiring Manager.

The Resume Service

A resume will serve as your gate pass for you to be able to land on the job that you are eying for. However, not all people are gifted with the ability of writing a responsive resume that will stand out among the rest hence there are resume service these days.

What are the benefits of going for resume service? Well, one thing that you can get from their service is the ability to create a resume that will excel above others without actually putting yourself in a lot of stress of looking for the right words to merge together towards your benefit. Of course, their works would come with a price but if you try to think about the benefit that you will get from their service, you will see that the price is not really something to fret about.

In looking for someone who can write your resume for you, it is wise to give her a complete background about your accomplishments and backgrounds. You may want to speak out your weaknesses and strengths so the one who will write for you will be able to put these information on your resume in the sense that your positive traits will overshadow your negative characters. If you wish to get the best out of their service, you should confirm first the reliability of such person so you would get the best out of their work. Of course since you are going to spare your cash, might as well get something that will make your spending worthy. Look around for someone who were given good reviews by other people who tried their service.

Jimmy Sweeney is president of CareerJimmy and author of the brand new, Amazing Resume Creator

<http://www.amazingresumecreator.com/> In just 10 minutes flat you can quickly and easily CREATE or UPDATE your resume without spending a lot of money. Just a few visits of your mouse turns an "average" resume into an AMAZING resume guaranteed to land you more hot job interviews next week. Learn how to stand out from the crowd of job seekers <http://www.amazingresumecreator.com/> and attract the attention of Hiring Manager.

A Resume Format

If you are making your resume, the first question that would probably pop up into your head is-what resume format should I follow? Well, with so many to choose from, you will really have a hard time looking for the right one to use.

Truth is, you can make use of whatever you like as long as such resume format will exude the sense of professionalism. Avoid the use of too fancy fonts or those that are too small since this will sacrifice the readability of the resume. Try to shun away from too many additions like underlines, bold fonts, and even italicized letters since this will lessen the sense of expertise of your work. You should also prevent the use of too many kinds of fonts, as much as possible stick to only one.

Put in mind that employers would often detect your own personality depending upon the resume format that you use hence it is only right to look for the kind of format that will match your personality. If you think that one format is fitted on you then you should not feel skeptical in using it. Now, if you can't find any then you should not lose your patience in looking because before the day ends, you will surely find the one that will give you a sense of satisfaction and contentment.

Looking for resume format is easy now because of the availability of information over the internet. All you have to do is to make a simple visit and you can expect to find the answers to all of your questions.

Jimmy Sweeney is president of CareerJimmy and author of the brand new, Amazing Resume Creator <http://www.amazingresumecreator.com/> In just 10 minutes flat you can quickly and easily CREATE or UPDATE your resume without spending a lot of money. Just a few visits of your mouse turns an "average" resume into an AMAZING resume guaranteed to land you more hot job interviews next week. Learn how to stand out from the crowd of job seekers <http://www.amazingresumecreator.com/> and attract the attention of Hiring Manager.

Talk About Your Resume

If you are trying to write a resume, you may have a hard time looking for the right words to make your work standout among the rest so you will be recognized by your employer. However, as you go along the process of writing, you may suddenly admit the fact that you are really not good in making one hence you start to crave for resume examples that may serve as a guide in your writing.

The good news is, there are a lot of resume examples that can be found in the internet. With this, you will not have any hard time in looking for the right one to match your needs. In fact, there are a lot of websites that would specialize on this service. You may want to try them and look for one which will best fit the requirement of the employer that you wish to work for.

As a general rule, always make sure that your resume is honest and clear as possible. Never dare to put up false facts about you just for the aim of stealing the attention of your employer. Doing this will cause you a lot of trouble especially if your employer will exert their effort in verifying the facts about you. Can you take the risk of not landing the job position and being ridiculed by people who got to know that you pretended to have accomplished something when in fact you did not? That said, practice honestly at all times, and this include when you are applying for a job.

Jimmy Sweeney is president of CareerJimmy and author of the brand new, Amazing Resume Creator <http://www.amazingresumecreator.com/> In just 10 minutes flat you can quickly and easily CREATE or UPDATE your resume without spending a lot of money. Just a few visits of your mouse turns an "average" resume into an AMAZING resume guaranteed to land you more hot job interviews next week. Learn how to stand out from the crowd of job seekers <http://www.amazingresumecreator.com/> and attract the attention of Hiring Manager.

Resume Writing Tips - Are Keywords Really Important in a Resume?

Working with scores of job seekers, the question about the importance of resume keywords often comes up. The answer, of course, is yes, but you must be strategic in how you go about incorporating them into the document and you must be selective in terms of the keywords you chose to include.

Why is this even an Issue?

Some of you may be wondering why this is a concern, as it is obvious to you that keywords must be used in a resume. However, many candidates feel that these buzzwords don't mean anything and that the hiring manager will say "so what" when reading their information. They are concerned that anyone can put a list of buzzwords together, especially if they do so in a separate competencies section in which they don't have to support the inclusion of those terms with any detail.

If this describes you, remember that the hiring manager is not the only one that will be reviewing your resume. In fact, they won't be the first to view it, as resumes must successfully pass through the HR screening process in most organizations. It is for this audience, the HR representative, that the keyword list is so essential. They will generally only spend between five and twenty seconds scanning each resume to determine whether a candidate should get passed along to the hiring manager. In that short window, they will not be able to read the resume, so they look at how your keywords match up with some of the requirements and preferences listed on the job posting.

Where Do I Place the Keywords?

Although having the keywords spread throughout your resume will generate hits on database searches, the HR folks won't have enough time to locate them in that manner. Instead, add a separate keywords section after your profile summary so that HR representatives can easily spot them and quickly scan through them.

What Keywords Do I Use?

Selecting your keywords appropriately is important. The best strategy is to review the content of the job posting to identify some of the language used, which will clue you in on the types of terms that the HR folks will be looking for on each candidate's resume. Also, consider the position you are pursuing and some of the most important attributes of a candidate in that type of job. Even if they are not included in the job posting, it may be beneficial to include them in your resume. One word of caution, however. Don't overdo it. Too many keywords will possibly turn off a prospective employer. Try to limit your number of buzzwords to about three or four lines of text, which may equate to between nine and sixteen terms.

If you have not been receiving calls from employers with your current resume, start by reviewing the keywords you have included in conjunction with the job descriptions you have posted for.

So who am I anyway? Why do I think my advice is so valuable?

My name is Stephen Van Vreede. My company is called No Stone Unturned, and I have spent 15 years on both sides of the corporate hiring experience. The short story is that I have an MBA in Marketing from Villanova University and a dual B.S. degree in Finance & Logistics from the University of Maryland. I am a certified professional resum頜 writer (CPRW) and a member of the Professional Association of Resume Writers and Career Coaches (PARW/CC). As I mentioned, I paid my dues in the corporate world eventually running a large-scale call center for a major truck rental company, and I have spent the past 7 years with No Stone Unturned, assisting job seekers in achieving their goals.

In February 2009, I launched a new group job hunting networking site: NoddlePlace.com. It is absolutely FREE to join, and you have access to everything on the site. Come check it out at NoddlePlace <http://www.noddleplace.com> . You can also follow me on Twitter <http://www.twitter.com/noddleplace> .

How to Assess a Resume Preparation Service

With the economy tanking and U.S. unemployment rising at almost unprecedented rates, resume writing services are popping up all over, trying to cash in on what looks like a great opportunity to make a few bucks. There's nothing wrong with entrepreneurial individuals knowing where their niche market it and going after it as they provide a solution to the needs at hand.

However, what we are really seeing is not a new group of talented individuals trying to fill a need in a niche market. We are seeing an influx of individuals who, for the most part, have no talent other than finding a way to make some quick money to pay their own bills.

Do you really need to pay to have your resume done? Frankly, in an economy like this, every job hunter out there needs an edge. They need as much professional help as they can afford to beat the competition. Much like an actor needs a good agent to land the coveted roles, a job seeker needs a great marketing tool - a resume - to land the coveted jobs.

Here are some easy tips on how to find the real experts out there and stay clear of anyone who can't provide you with the talent, expertise and experience you need to help you shine in an economy such as this.

Do they have a website? Frequently the ones who advertise on boards such as Craigslist or Backpage, etc., don't have a site to be referred to.

If they have a website, is it professionally done? Is there contact information, pricing, and a year they started in business?

What are the qualifications of the person / service? Don't jump just because someone says they were an HR Manager, head hunter, or recruiter. Believe it or not, these people are not trained in the science of resume writing! Sure, they can spot a good resume, but they can probably spot a good book, too. Reading a good book doesn't mean they can write a good book. Same with a resume.

What are the qualifications you should look for? The best qualified individuals are actually certified by the National Resume Writers Association. Certification entails a very lengthy study course and an equally lengthy and detailed testing procedure. Think SATs. It's costly, too. This is not some run of the mill association that just anyone can sign up for. Look for the NRWA blue logo on any site that claims to have extensive experience.

What are they charging? This is an excellent example of "you get what you pay for". A great resume can easily reach the $500 range. Is it worth it? That's up to you! But when you are assessing what you get for your money, keep in mind that a real resume preparation service spends a considerable amount of time working with you one-on-one. It's much more detailed than submitting a current resume, filling out a form, selecting PayPal at checkout, and waiting a day or so for a completed resume. A professional, experienced service puts someone in charge of your account, understands your past, your goals, and knows how to translate all that into a language that will be targeted directly at the companies you are interested in working for.

What happens with a lower priced resume service? You get less of the personal attention, if you get any at all. Chances are you do everything online and have no idea who is doing your resume or what the resulting product will look like. They work with your present resume, make some changes, do some spell checking and editing, and in many instances your new resume doesn't look all that different from the one you had before. If you're looking in the under $100 price range, this is about what you can reasonably expect.

What about guarantees? In all honesty, it's difficult to "guarantee" a resume simply because people will always blame the resume service if they are having trouble finding a job. A guarantee in this particular industry doesn't mean they guarantee you any type of job success. It usually means you'll be happy with the end product, and some even promise in writing that you will get at least phone calls and interviews. A good guarantee simply means that you should at least end up with a quality document that effectively portrays your experience, abilities and career goals.

Marie Duffo is past owner and President of:

South FLA Staffing, National Affordable Staffing - employment agencies that specialized in sales and marketing executives' recruitment and placement.

Sitters to Go, a leading US Nanny agency with offices in Boston, Miami, Chicago and San Francisco.

Career Options, a Boston based consulting firm that specialized in outplacement and vocational testing and services.

Professional Resumes, Inc., Boston and Miami based service for executive level marketing managers.

Marie now owns Miami Writing Machine and is a full time writer and copy editor specializing in business topics that focus on employment, staffing and career advice. She can be found at http://miamiwritingmachine.books.officelive.com

Follow her on Twitter: http://twitter.com/MiamiWriting

Resumes - Best Objective Statement and Summary Section to Get the Interview

Remember, there are no hard and fast rules about what needs to be in your resume, or what format you should use. Whatever gets the employer to call you for an interview, is great.

1. OBJECTIVE STATEMENT

The best time to use an objective statement is when you're switching job functions and/or industries. Without an objective statement, employers expect that you are applying for the same job as your current job, and that you are looking in the same industry. So for example, if you last worked in the construction industry as an accountant, and you're applying for an accountant position at a college, employers get really confused and throw your resume away.

The same thing can happen if your last job was working as a business analyst in the financial services industry, and you're applying for a project manager position, in financial services. These jobs are often very similar, but again, hiring managers are looking for the easiest decision, and may just throw your resume away.

In either case, the best thing to do is "hook" the manager by letting them know exactly what you're looking for, AND telling them about your best qualification:

Objective: A __________ position in the __________ industry, using my __________ skills

This statements works really, really well because it only takes 1 or 2 seconds for employers to see why they should hire you, and practically forces them to read the rest of your resume.

2. SUMMARY SECTION

A really good, well written, summary section allows you to be considered for the job, based on the strength of your entire career. Without it, employers will base their decision solely on your last position. So, if you have worked at more than one job, and your previous experience is valuable and relevant to your target position, then you need to use a summary section.

A summary section is really valuable when you want a job like the one you had two or three jobs ago. Imagine that you worked in computer support, later as a software tester, and now you're a computer programmer. You decide that you hate being a programmer, and you loved being a software tester. You can use your summary section to "position yourself" as a tester with some development skills, which is always in high demand.

Ready to learn more about how to get more interviews <http://www.magneticresume.com> for each resume you send out?

Download my FREE 12-page report, "Anatomy of a Perfect Resume," at http://www.magneticresume.com so you can learn:

* The 4 most common deadly mistakes that people make and how to fix them!
* How to create the perfect Career Objective & Career Summary sections
* How to maximize your resume so you're the candidate your next boss wants to meet!

Scott Shane Holt has seen it all while hiring over 100 people, in good times and bad, and as an executive coach helping managers and other professionals accelerate their careers.

Resumes - 3 Must Use Tactics For Professionals Without a Degree

I have a little known secret for you. Lack of a college degree is rarely a deal breaker for getting the job. In fact, most employers couldn't care less if you have a degree or not, as long as you have an employment history that shows you can do the job.

However, you may have a limiting belief about not having a degree. Maybe you work in a competitive environment where all your peers have degrees. You could have been taught from an early age that college is the key to a happy, successful life. Maybe you really wanted to get a degree, but couldn't go to school, or finish school, because of a very good reason. Perhaps you have been turned down because "Sorry, you don't have a degree."

In any case, you have managed to come this far, and develop "great history, great experience, and a proven record" without a degree, so you know that it is possible.

As a professional without a college degree, keep these things in mind:

1. IT MAY MATTER MORE TO YOU THAN IT DOES TO EMPLOYERS

Have you noticed that the educational requirements are usually at the bottom of the ad? That's because they are usually tacked on by human resources. I have written 100 job requirements in my career, and I've never asked for a degree. However, HR will sometimes add the requirement before the job is posted.

Employers, especially hiring managers, are interested in your ability to do the job and your past experience. That's why once you have job experience, education is listed at the bottom of your resume.

2. HOW YOU APPLY CAN MAKE A BIG DIFFERENCE

Some companies require you to fill out a form when you apply online. If you fill out the form, there's no way to downplay the lack of a degree, because you're forced to select "No College Degree." You can bypass this step completely if you network your way to the hiring manager. Talk to all of your friends, use LinkedIn, or cold-call the manager if you can figure out who they are.

Once the manager likes you, you're in, because the hiring manager is the decision maker, not HR. And they rarely ask about your college degree.

3. FOCUS ON YOUR STRONGEST QUALIFICATIONS

Think of your resume as your greatest hits, not your complete collection. Your greatest hits are your great history, the great experience that you have accumulated, and your proven record. Highlight these attributes and downplay your lack of a degree.

If you have enough experience, write a two-page resume. Most people never read the second page (so your education won't even cross their mind). If you attended college for any amount of time, list the college, and your major, but no graduation date. Enroll in an adult college degree program at night and take one class a semester. Actively pursuing a degree will never be held against you.

Ready to learn more about how to get more interviews <http://www.magneticresume.com> for each resume you send out?

Download my FREE 12-page report, "Anatomy of a Perfect Resume," at http://www.magneticresume.com so you can learn:

The 4 most common deadly mistakes that people make and how to fix them!

How to create the perfect Career Objective & Career Summary sections

How to maximize your resume so you're the candidate your next boss wants to meet!

Scott Shane Holt has seen it all while hiring over 100 people, in good times and bad, and as an executive coach helping managers and other professionals accelerate their careers.

Administrative Assistant CVs - How to Write Them Effectively

Because of the competitive nature of job markets, a single application for an administrative assistant position can draw hundreds of applicants. As a result, employers typically scan resumes in mere seconds, usually about thirty seconds. For this reason, your administrative assistant CV must have all the right features that will encourage the reader to read through your resume. Typically, badly written CVs end up in the bin so it is vital to avoid the pitfalls when writing your own administrative assistant resume.

You should write your administrative assistant CV in 2 pages. This should be sufficient for you to highlight relevant administrative skills, expertise, experience and qualifications. If you have been in an administrative position for a considerable period of time and have taken up positions with increasing responsibility, you may require more than 2 pages to fully document your career. This is acceptable so long as the information is relevant.

When compiling your administrative assistant CV, keep the layout and format simple so that the presentation is easy on the eye. Your CV should be written in black with Arial or Times Roman font and size 10 or 12 for the content. Your heading should be written in size 14 or 16 and the document should be consistent both in layout, font style and size.

It is important that the reader understand your career goal quickly from your resume. You should therefore start your CV with a persuasive profile briefly detailing your background in administration and your objective. Your professional profile should be kept to a short paragraph of no more than 3 or 4 sentences. Your introductory professional profile statement should be followed by a bulleted list of your key skills relevant to administrative job positions. The list should contain no more than 8 short lines. If you are entering an administrative position for the first time, then your key skills should include relevant transferable skills such as attention to detail, organizational skills and ability to work accurately under pressure. Your key skills summary should typically include the following:

* A methodical approach to work
* Your organizational skills
* Your ability to work proactively within a team setting
* Your ability to work effectively on your own initiative
* Good communication and interpersonal skills
* Sound computer skills and competent typing ability
* Your attention to detail and ability to work accurately
* Ability to work to deadlines and work effectively under pressure

If you are entering an administrative post with no previous experience, perhaps because you are a recent graduate, then you should add details of your education and training before your work experience, highlighting areas that are directly applicable to your remit in administration such as English, numerical qualifications and computer literacy certifications. If on the other hand you have amassed previous experience as an administrator, then your professional work experience should precede your education and qualifications. When presenting your work experience, try to describe the skills you used in your remits and how the position helped you hone those skills further, along with other skills you acquired within the post.

Your CV should be written in the third person with minimal use of "I" in your document. Also, always mention dates, names of employers and names of educational institutions attended. You should also highlight achievements and other significant results that bear relevance to a position in administration.

Richard Blake is a Professional CV writer <http://www.professional-cv-writingservices.co.uk> catering for school leavers, graduates, and professionals up to senior exectives and CEOs. Services also include medical doctor CV <http://www.professional-cv-writingservices.co.uk/cvs/medical-cv.html> preparation along with cover letters.

Rework Your Resume For Today's Market

Though the outlook for employment may seem grim with reports of companies executing mass layoffs, it doesn't necessarily mean there are no jobs to be found. A simple search through Internet employment databases may reveal many vacancies, opportunities for you to stand out among others with your expertise. In order to get noticed and get the interview, however, it is important to have an updated, concise resume of your qualifications.

Take a look at your current resume. How long has it been since you last revised it? On average, a person may only update his vitae once a year, if at that. Often, a resume becomes an afterthought while one is employed, and unfortunately is hastily retooled when it is needed. So as not to be caught off-guard, it may be best to pull out your resume every three months or so to see what is relevant in your career path that needs to be recorded. Remember, a resume is not just a list of jobs you have held, but life experiences. A resume is a record of your continuing education through employment, community achievements, and your employable skills.

Have you learned any new skills in your present job that may benefit you during a new search? Work with new computer applications and others skills should be pointed out here. Larger companies emphasizing a sense of community among their employees may search for well-rounded candidates, so if you have done any recent volunteer work be sure to mention it. It is also a good idea to refresh your references, and list somebody who has worked with you in the last six months or so who can vouch for you during a job search.

For years the rule of thumb with resumes has been to keep everything to one page. If you have much information to share, it can be challenge to limit your experiences. Including a URL leading to a more detailed vitae may help an employer see a fuller picture of who you are and what you can bring to the company.

As you work, and as you search for work, remember to keep your resume current and relevant for the jobs you seek. This simple document is your first introduction to a potential employer, so have it ready to make a good impression.

Kathryn Lively is a freelance writer who specializes in articles on jobs in Hampton Roads <http://donrichard.com/> and Virginia Beach website design <http://www.ciniva.com> .

Common Illegal Questions You Shouldn't Be Asked During a Job Interview

Have you ever had a job interview where you wondered why in the world the prospective employer was asking certain questions that you thought were strange? If you thought they were strange, then you were probably right. There are certain questions that shouldn't be asked during a job interview. As a matter of fact, federal law prohibits an employer from asking questions that are not relevant to the job. All questions should be related to the job and not used to gather personal information.

Here are some of the questions that you should not be asked during an interview, but employers tend to do it anyway:

? What is your ethnicity?
? What is your sexual orientation?
? What is your religion?
? Do you attend church services regularly?
? Where were you born?
? How old are you?
? Do you have any disabilities?

? Are you married?
? Do you have children?

All of these questions have nothing to do with the job. The employer may ask if you have adequate transportation to get back and forth to work, but that is relevant to the job. It is relevant because your job depends on you being able to be there. The employer wants to make sure you can fulfill your obligation each day.

As for whether or not you have children or you are married, those questions are not relevant to the job. Most adults do have children and most adults do have a significant other. There are also many adults who don't have these things. Employers are not allowed to discriminate against you because you do have children.

Actually, an employer is not allowed to discriminate against you for anything at all. Many good candidates could be passed up due to discrimination. Everyone is to have an equal chance at getting the job regardless of their personal circumstances.

Unfortunately, there are still employers asking these questions and they are getting by with it. They have been known to ask questions such as, "Will your children get in the way of your job responsibilities?" They may even ask, "Do you have adequate childcare so that you can carry out your job duties?" These questions are not needed. Now, an employer may ask a question, such as "Are you physically capable to carry out the job duties?" This is a viable question for the fact that some jobs require heavy lifting or have other physical demands. If a person is not able to carry out those physical demands, then they may find that performing their job is very difficult. If someone says they are able to fulfill the physical demands, but they don't, then they could lose their job. This question cannot be considered a "disability" question.

If you find that you are being asked illegal questions in a job interview, it may be in your best interest to turn down a job offer. If they want to know why, there is nothing wrong with telling them that their questions were too personal. If they are going to ask you such questions during a job interview, then it is hard to tell how personal things would get when actually doing the job. You could be treading on shallow water and find yourself in a job that you would not like.

When you call an employer out on their illegal questions, you may be opening their eyes to what it is they are doing. Then again, you may not be. Just know that an employer that asks illegal questions is not exactly the type of employer you want to dedicate your time to.

English School offering to free English Lessons online <http://www.englishlink.com/freelesson_ENG_HTML.asp> to help the students to improve their communication skills. Also visit our resume format <http://www.englishlink.com/JobsIndex_ENG_HTML.asp> section.

How to Make Your Internship Cover Letter Standout and Not Become a Trashcan Liner

When looking for an internship your cover letter is even more important than your resume. Every year companies receive hundreds of resumes from eager college students wanting to gain "experience" by working as an intern for their company. Moreover, every year hundreds of students are passed over because no one takes the time to read their resume.

Don't let your resume become a trashcan liner! Here are a few quick tricks to get the attention you need in order to get into the door of any company.

1. Don't be shy or humble SELL YOURSELF!

2. If you know someone at the company include their name in your cover letter. Make sure you call them first to let them know you want to intern at their company, NETWORK!

3. If you have won an award or gotten recognition in the field you wish to intern, include that in your cover letter.

4. Intern at companies that pertain to your major, Yes, It's dumb to mention but there is always that one person who thinks a biology major entitles them to Intern at CBS.

5. Include in your cover letter what YOU have to offer the company. Answer the "What's in it for me" question before it's asked.

A well-written cover letter will open countless doors for you. The experience you gain as an intern is priceless. Don't forget to Network during your Internship. The person you meet today may be the person who hires you tomorrow.

It's important to understand the cover letter is only a small part of getting that perfect internship.

For more information on how to get the internship you deserve please read: Internship With Dream Employer <http://www.easyinternshipguide.com/bagging-that-internship-with-your-dream-employer.php> today. http://www.easyinternshipguide.com is dedicated to helping people find a great internship that will launch a successful career.

Free Cover Letter Samples - Yes, There is Help For Writing Your Cover Letter

Cover letters have become a standard practice for most professional jobs these days. You usually send one along with your resume as a chance to sell yourself by highlighting your skills and experience for the job. However, many people don't know the first thing about writing a good one.

The good news is that there's tons of help out there in the form of free cover letter samples. All you have to do is go to Google, or your favorite search engine, and search for "free cover letter samples" and you'll be presented with hundreds of sites that offer the free samples.

Now obviously, you'll still need to do a little work to find a good sample, as well as rewrite it to fit your needs. Follow the steps below to select your samples and customize them to fit your needs:

Step 1: Do a search for "free cover letter samples" on Google or your favorite search engine and browse through the results. Look for a sample that fits with the job you are applying for.

Step 2: Copy and paste one or two of the samples into your word processing program and begin to edit it. At this step, you can change the obvious things like names, addresses and companies.

Step 3: Now you'll want to edit the sample further and make it your own. You can do this by changing the experience mentioned to your own experience. Also, try and use the company's name in the letter to show that it's personalized to them. You also might want to take a look at the company's website and see if you can relate any of your experience to their industry.

Step 4: Go back through the edits and rewrite the entire letter to make sure all sentences and paragraphs flow together well.

Step 5: In this final step, you want to print your cover letter and proofread it to ensure there are no mistakes. This is very important, as one mistake could cause an employer to overlook you. Once you're done proofing and it's error-free, it's time to send it and get the job!

Greg Quigley publishes Qcomnet.com, a business writing samples site that includes free cover letter samples <http://www.qcomnet.com/free_cover_letter_sample.htm> . Qcomnet.com also provides other types of writing samples in addition to its cover letter samples <http://www.qcomnet.com/free_cover_letter_sample.htm> , such as sponsorship letter samples and radio commercial scripts.

Resume Mania - Are You Making Any of These 3 Deadly Resume Mistakes?

Many people who need a resume fast don't realize writing it can be a trap and end up blowing it.

Think about 3 of the deadly resume mistakes and pitfalls and what you should do about them.

Mistake #1: Believing the resume is a job application. You are imprinted at birth with what others believe a resume should look like. They have made up your mind that you should bare all: everything should be dated; give pay rates for past "6" jobs; insert address and phone number of former employers; show supervisor name and title; and list references. Not good.

What to do instead: The purpose of a resume is to get an interview, not to get a job. Focus. Like a golf game, fewer keystrokes the better. Remove clutter caused by too many dates, bullets, phone numbers, addresses, and names of supervisors and references. Don't repeat the same word or phrase again and again, job to job. More white space, the better.

Mistake #2: Not realizing a resume is a legal document. About 75% of all resumes contain "errors" and "inaccuracies." We call them lies, fudging, bending, overstatement, and cheating. Harsh? Vetting is in. Skating is out. You will be found out. You won't be hired. If you are hired, later you will be fired.

What to do instead: Beware. Here's a test. Are you willing to send your finished resume to your former employer for her comments? If not, cut out the stuff you don't want her to see. Fact checkers can forward your resume to former employers.

Mistake #3: Worrying that selling you is not cool; too bold. Female candidates undersell their background, experience, skills, and abilities. Google Dr. Patricia Heim, the authority. Unless you have an agent, "If it is to be it is up to U!"

What to do instead: Your resume is a marketing document disguised as a resume. Yes it has "sell" in it and it should. Proudly display your expertise that matches employer needs. Emphasize results in statements of accomplishment that relate to job requirements. More results the better.

And now I'd like to invite you to claim your Free Access to live job search teleseminars inspired by Job Angels co-hosted by veteran career coaches (on the phone and on the web, your choice) every Sunday 9PM US EST when you visit http://www.resumesteve.com/

You'll get as much time as you need to jump-start or restart your job search and for a change, have fun doing it. No charge.

Stephen Q Shannon The Free Teleseminar Resume Guy

Resume Writing - Think Outside the Job

When resume writing, you need to think 'outside the job.' We all obtain skills and abilities from job experience and education. We also get them from outside the work environment and those can be as valuable to employers. Many of these were not learned on the job or demonstrated for an employer. This does not diminish their value and therefore you should take stock of your assets that might not have been obtained or proven in traditional employment positions.

Here is an example:

* Strong negotiating skills obtained from experience of bringing rival gangs together to work side by side for completion of a city beautification project

That is a testament to negotiating skills. Can you imagine any business negotiating that would be tougher than that?

How about this resume writing example:

* Resourceful and quick ability to prioritize tasks proven by choosing targets based on level of threat while under fire as a soldier in the Iraq war.

This one sentence makes me want to hire this person.

Here is another:

* Perform well under pressure and have responsive decision making skills demonstrated by administering CPR to unconscious swimmer pulled from the ocean. (She was revived.)

This would be another great person to have around.

OK so maybe you haven't been to war or saved anyone's life. Skills and abilities can be developed or demonstrated in everyday situations also.

Examples:

* Management and leadership required to supervise church group of twenty seven middle school students on two five hour bus rides and entire weekend retreat including six hour raft trip. (Everyone survived.)

* Patience and empathy established during volunteer work with developmentally disabled children.

* Proven management and organizational talent developed by running a family household of five for a pilot husband for eleven years.

* Motivational skills expanded as the Captain of college soccer team with a 36-6 record.

When resume writing you can include relevant statements from unconventional situations to show additional skills you possess to shore up areas where you are weak in job experience. Employers appreciate employees with strong skills and look for those in candidates. That you obtained and exhibit desirable and relevant employee attributes in circumstances outside the job shows you are a learner and responsible.

Job Cover Letter Sample - Follow Up

So you have done the job interview Now it's been several weeks and you and neither a peep nor beep from the company. Did they reject your application? Maybe they did. Or maybe they were just flooded with applications and overlooked yours.

It's always good to follow up your case. Use the job cover letter sample for follow ups below. Doing a follow up increases your chances of a review.

Some companies may have specific job application procedures, such as deadlines and on-site exams. Be sure to customize this job cover letter sample to the one you're applying for.

Job Cover Letter Sample: Follow Up

XXXX (name)
XXX (address)

XXX (city state zip)
000 (telephone and email)

day month year

Re: Follow Up to Job Application Ref No. 12345
XXX
XXX

Dear Mr. Mrs_____

It has been 2 weeks since our interview. Thank you for giving me the opportunity to discuss employment options with you. I would like to reiterate my interest in the yoga instructor position you have available.

Since our interview, I have learned that your school is now expanding its curriculum to include Ayurveda medicine. I was pleased to know this as I have been an ardent practitioner of the ayurvedic discipline for many years, and obtained a certificate from the Ayurveda Institute of California fourteen months ago.

I strongly believe that Hatha Yoga and Ayurveda complement each other as well as other Eastern holistic healing disciplines. It is my hope to be able to share these precious gifts with our community through your school.

I look forward to hearing from you once again. If you need any more information, please don't hesitate to contact me.

Sincerely,

XXX

Mark Mattey is a writer and entrepreneur. To learn more about Job Cover Letter Sample <http://www.coverlettersthatkill.com> or Quality Job Cover Letter <http://www.coverlettersthatkill.com> , visit his website.

What an Employer is Looking For in Your CV

When writing your Curriculum Vitae it is really tempting to make yourself out to be the coolest, most interesting person on the planet. But the reality is that most employers are not actually looking to appoint the coolest person in the world, they are looking for someone with the necessary skills, experience and attributes, that are required for the position that they are trying to fill.

Usually, employers have an idea of the kind of person that they want to fill a vacancy. That person may, for example, be required to be very hard working, trustworthy, a team player, able to cope with stress and so on. So your Curriculum Vitae should reflect these type of skills.

If you are sending your Curriculum Vitae to a recruitment agency because you are looking for a temping job, then you should be aware that your Curriculum Vitae should still be as professionally produced as possible.

One thing that all employers will be looking for on your Curriculum Vitae is a spelling mistake. You need to make sure that your Curriculum Vitae has none, because many employers will think that your work is simply sloppy if you cannot even be bothered to spell check your Curriculum Vitae.

Your Curriculum Vitae also needs to demonstrate to the employer that you are a balanced, well-rounded individual, so they will be looking for someone who has interests, hobbies and something of a life apart from studying or work, or both. But don't make your hobbies sound too extreme or weird, since this may actually backfire on you, with the employer assuming you are a bit strange.

One final consideration to bear in mind is that whatever you put on your Curriculum Vitae, you should be mindful of the fact that the employer may pick up on it at interview and ask you for more details at interview, so make sure that you have not embroidered your experience too much; keep everything factual!

Recruitment agency <http://www.tate.co.uk/recruitment-agency.aspx> solutions spanning temping, temps, contract and permanent in London we specialise in placement and recruitment in the Uk from PA Jobs <http://www.tate.co.uk/job-listing/personal-assistants-jobs/JobCategoryIDs/1.aspx> Receptionist Jobs, Secretarial Jobs, Admin Jobs, Customer Service Jobs and Data Entry Jobs

Is Your Resume Right For the Job Market Fight?

In a downward spiraling economy where the unemployment rate continues to soar, your resume can have tremendous power and be the difference between you and the other candidate getting called for an interview. If crafted effectively as a marketing tool, this critical document that is sometimes under-rated can make a tremendous impact on your job search. Here are 10 tips to get you started with developing a stellar impact-producing resume that will put you yards ahead of the competition.

1. Determine who you are professionally and where you are trying to go in your career. Craft your resume based on these definitions of yourself.

2. Envision how you want to be perceived by your prospective employer. Are you a change agent? What about a project leader? The top 2 steps will give your resume focus and direction, meeting your goals instead of a chronological record of past jobs.

3. Communicate your value. Make a list of your quantifiable achievements and the impact of the results. How have you saved the company money? Hiring managers would love for you to transfer your track record to their organization.

4. Highlight your successes and relevant qualifications. Are you a change agent? Show how you plan to be an asset at your next place of employment.

5. Save the minute details for the interview. You know you can't tell everything. Just include enough relevant information for the hiring manager to say, "I must meet this individual."

6. Instead of regurgitating your job description on paper (telling), try advertising your accomplishments (selling).

7. Use powerful action words to advertise your past accomplishments. It's not what you say; it's how you say it.

8. Include key words that pertain to the job to which you are applying. This is also beneficial if your resume is electronically

scanned who search for specific words that demonstrate your knowledge, skills, and abilities.

9. Proof read your resume. Do not rely on your computer's spell check feature since it will not identify correct words used in the wrong context.

10. Market your new document by networking, using referrals and online job searches. Remember, the majority of jobs are not advertised.

Bonus Tip - Remember, your resume will be scanned for only about 10 seconds. To win an interview, you must ensure that pertinent information is communicated in this short amount of time. This way, you will make it easy for the reviewers to see exactly what you want them to see and your marketing tool will achieve its intended purpose - an interview.

Master Resume-writer and Resume Strategist Claudia A. Samuels Newton is the President and CEO of Rewarding Resume Services (http://www.rewardingresumes.com). Claudia has a Masters of Management in Human Resource Management degree and a Bachelors of Science degree in Business Administration. With over 20 years of industry experience, she has served hundreds of satisfied clients. Her speaking engagements include being a featured guest on WLTX TV in Columbia, SC and serving as a resume-writing consultant for higher education institutions in her community. Samuels-Newton provides online instruction in Communications as an Adjunct Faculty member for the University of Phoenix Online. She also serves in a management role at BlueChoice HealthPlan, a subsidiary of BlueCross BlueShield of SC.

Stop Gambling! Your Resume is Too Important to Leave Up to Chance

A resume is a valuable marketing tool that when well crafted, maximizes your chances of being seen by prospective employers who will invite you for an interview. While there are indeed stories of people who were hired based on just their resume, the reality is your resume does not get you a job. The sole purpose of your resume is to get you interviewed by the hiring manager. How will you measure up?

Since the resume is such a crucial part of your job search, it is imperative that you make the necessary efforts to ensure that you get rewarding results. Every day, many job applicants take the risk of writing their own resume. It is a risk that is too expensive to take when there is so much at stake. You have already invested so much into getting a quality education. Why diminish your qualifications by not further investing into marketing yourself? Usually, you will only get as much as you put in.

Think of all the channels that your resume must go through. If you are applying to a midsize to large company, a recruiter in the Human Resources Office will be the first to go through the hundreds or perhaps even thousands of responses. When the hiring manager posts a vacancy, he or she usually submits a job description to the recruiter. The job description is made up of categories such as: Required Education, Minimum Requirements, and Preferred Requirements etc. The recruiter sorts this enormous stack of responses into the accepted or rejected piles based on the criteria of the job description. Of course, their decision will be based on what they quickly scan within the first minute.

Needless to say, the rejected pile goes straight to the garbage. The accepted pile will go through another round of scrutiny to pick out the top 10 or 20, depending on the request of the hiring manager. A weak resume will not survive this round. The recruiter will then submit the finalists to the hiring manager, who again will assess your resume in detail to see if you have the necessary qualifications. In my role as a hiring manager, I have literally picked resumes apart at this stage, throwing some in the garbage at a glance.

Given the aforementioned process, it is wise for the serious job hunter to leave the writing in the hands of a professional resume writer. The writer should not be one who creates imaginary and farfetched claims that you will never be able to substantiate in an interview. Remember even if you do get a job based on lies, you may get terminated further down the road when the lie catches up with you. There are several new employees who listed phony degrees on their resumes, who were shown to the door once the verification process took place.

A professional writer will extract your factual related job experience and credentials along with your accomplishments and use them to present you as someone who can bring significant value to a prospective employer. Your writer will also use the correct format (Chronological, Functional, or Combination) and design to arrange your key selling points in the most compelling way. Furthermore, your professional writer knows how to use strategy to present job applicants who have aspects working against them such as job-hopping, little experience, or no college degree. There are also those candidates who need special attention such as converting their resumes from military to civilian or those who desire a career change. Does the applicant overstate their achievements to the point of being ludicrous or does he downplay his qualifications in the name of modesty? Will your resume make you seem overqualified and a potential threat to the hiring manger who may think you will one day get his job?

The bottom line is your resume is too important of a document to leave in the hands of an amateur or to use resume books to copy lines that do not accurately reflect who you are and what you have to offer. A copy and paste job is also a far cry from the customized and personalized document that your writer will prepare for you. When a professional resume writer writes your resume, rest assured that he or she is incorporating strategy, expertise, and marketing techniques to present you at your very best on paper.

Importance of Preparing a Resume

Whenever an individual is preparing a resume for any position, you want to make a first impression that will be everlasting. If a person wants their resume to make a impression on a potential employer, your resume needs to get attention, and remain on the top of the list when an employer reads all the resumes.

Any person only has 1 chance and 1 chance only on making a great first impression. If a person fails at the 1 and only shot, then they can never have a chance again for that first impression. When a perspective employer see's you, , you need to show dignity, honor, and respect. Whenever a person is preparing a resume, you should want that resume to always to be on the cutting edge, but at the same time show your skills to the future employer, and show them how valuable you could be for the business.

A resume should always stick out, and be put together the correct way. The resume should be written were a person can understand it well. It should include only information that is useful. Always group all categories together. When grouping categories together, a person should keep their career objective separate from everything else. When summarizing their skills, put the expert skills that you have acquired at the top. The work experience should start with the most recent. The education, computer skills, and references should be kept separate.

When preparing a resume, a person always needs to tell the truth on their resume. Be honest, and don't exaggerate on anything on your resume. If you try to stretch the truth on anything, you will be found out. When a potential employer is looking for someone new, they want always want a truthful individual. The want an individual that is great with customers, trustworthy, and able to be at work on their scheduled days and be on time. On your resume always double check for spelling and grammar errors. This is very important for the 1st impression. A employer won't see you physically at first, but they will see your resume.

After an appropriate time has passed after submitting your resume, give a phone call to follow up , or give a visit to a prospective employer. This will show them that you are interested in the position they are offering. Remember that 1st impression is very important, and can go a long way in the job search.

Rodney Todd is part of a top internet marketing team of mentors, and has a passion for helping others achieve their goals, dreams and aspirations. To learn more about Rodney Todd go to http://www.christmentor.com

INDEX*

V

W

Breinigsville, PA USA
18 August 2009

222537BV00001BB/1/P

9 781921 644061